the accidental landlord

the keys to letting out your own property with complete peace of mind

DANIEL LEES & MARTINA LEES

Praise for the authors

'Many like to paint themselves as experts on the housing market, but few really make the cut. In *The Accidental Landlord*, Martina and Daniel, true experts, share their deep knowledge and extensive experience of the rental market. A charming read and essential guide for new investors.'

Johnny Morris, head of research at Countrywide, Britain's biggest estate agency

'A well laid out, easy to read and understand road map which will help you navigate your way through the often complex and highly regulated field of letting your property. It is a reference tool which will reduce the stress of letting your home to a complete stranger.'

Chris Cooper, co-founder of the Tenant Tax campaign, which has sued the government over buy-to-let tax changes with the help of Cherie Blair (crowdjustice.co.uk/case/tenanttax), and owner of 15 buy-to-let properties

'A must-read for any landlord wanting a step-by-step guide on how to rent out and manage a property yourself. Full of practical advice, tips and some humour along the way.'

Jo Eccles, managing director of the buying agency Sourcing Property and weekly property columnist for *The Metro* newspaper

'The UK rental market is dominated by accidental landlords, many of whom struggle to keep on top of their responsibilities. This book will provide an invaluable guide to help accidental landlords be confident, knowledgeable and professional landlords, which is good news for them, and great news for their tenants.'

Matt Hutchinson, director of house and flatshare site SpareRoom.co.uk

'Renting out a London property is a course of action many of our members choose when moving out of London. Becoming a landlord might initially seem like an easy option, but renting out your much-loved family home can be really daunting. This book will be a fantastic aid, ensuring the paperwork is up to scratch and all eventualities are considered. Martina has an effortless style, writing in a clear and approachable manner, and Daniel adds industry-specific knowledge with his years of experience in dealing with lettings, landlords and tenants. It's an informative book that will quickly prove invaluable to many accidental landlords.'

Belinda Aspinall, founder of LifeafterLondon.com, an advice forum on moving out of the capital

'A very readable book which helped me navigate my way in new and unfamiliar territory. I found the personal anecdotes really brought the book to life and made it feel very relevant to me.'

Susan Peacock, founder of LiveWorkWell consultancy and first-time landlord

'The must-have property guide for any accidental or intended landlord. To the point, with no blabber, Daniel and Martina's book is packed with useful advice that will sharpen even the seasoned landlord. Essential if you have just bought or are about to buy your first rental property, yet it will lift your game if you have been around the block in the buy-to-let industry.'

Eugene Brazelle, director of Global Invest property brokers

'Daniel and Martina confidently clear a path through the property jungle, pointing out all the lions and tigers who, yes, might kill you along the way! If you are brave enough to join the trip, it is going to change your life.'

Jonathan Moss, founder of Moss and Co estate agents and property professional since 1992

'I've been renting out properties in the UK for 10 years and I thought I knew it all. Not so! Practical, humorous and easy to digest, *The Accidental Landlord* is a must read for existing landlords and anyone considering getting into the rental game.'

Matt Marks, business intelligence architect and experienced landlord

RETHINK PRESS

First published in Great Britain 2016
by Rethink Press (www.rethinkpress.com)

© Copyright Daniel Lees and Martina Lees

All rights reserved. No part of this publication may be reproduced, stored in or introduced into a retrieval system, or transmitted, in any form, or by any means (electronic, mechanical, photocopying, recording or otherwise) without the prior written permission of the publisher.

The right of Daniel Lees and Martina Lees to be identified as the authors of this work has been asserted by them in accordance with the Copyright, Designs and Patents Act 1988.

This book is sold subject to the condition that it shall not, by way of trade or otherwise, be lent, resold, hired out, or otherwise circulated without the publisher's prior consent in any form of binding or cover other than that in which it is published and without a similar condition including this condition being imposed on the subsequent purchaser.

Contents

Plan

Property

People

Paperwork

Practicals

Conclusion

Foreword

We Brits are a home-loving nation. Our patriotism is not wrapped up in a flag or an anthem, but in our obsession with bricks and mortar. We're hooked on property-led growth. It is boundless. Expensive. Addictive. Yet in almost all cases we are mere amateurs.

We spend more money taking out a mortgage than anything else – and yet, probably take a fraction of the time it takes us to research a weekend break, what school to send our kids to or even simply finding a local yoga class to suit. And, thanks to crisis within the housing industry, more and more of us are so nervous to ever relinquish our hold on the property ladder that we find ourselves accidentally becoming landlords as we let out our own homes.

Then there's the semi-pro landlords. Since the birth of the buy-to-let mortgage in 1996, buy-to-let investments have outstripped every other major asset class. Every £1 used for a 25% deposit in 1996 would have been worth over £13 by 2013 – compared to only £3 in shares, and less than £2 in cash. So, as savings rates fall further and pensions fail to deliver the promised payouts, property is once more the go-to buy offering the (potential) twin rewards of income and profit. Get it right and the rewards are golden. Get it wrong and you could go broke.

Don't think you can just muddle along. You will need help. It is now more expensive than ever to enter the buy-to-let market – and it is more rigorously regulated and taxed. This where Martina and Daniel come in. They've been there, done it, made some mistakes and learned all the right lessons. They have done all the hard work so you don't have to. Read this before you even think of letting your home out. Read it again before you start dreaming of amassing your own portfolio or comparing the relative merits of Milton Keynes vs Liverpool, flats vs houses, sharers vs students.

The Accidental Landlord is the best guide to being a landlord I've read. It will answer all the questions you didn't even know you had to ask.

Good luck.

Helen Davies

Home editor, *The Sunday Times*

Introduction

If you're about to let out a property for the first time – especially if it's your own home – a million questions are likely to be racing through your mind. Who can you trust to look after it? What if the tenants stop paying rent, or a pipe bursts at midnight? Where do you start? Should you repaint? Re-do the bathroom? Rent it out at all when the government is making it so much harder for buy-to-lets?

It all boils down to peace of mind.

Perhaps you've just bought your first property investment. In the seven years since the financial crisis, buy-to-let mortgages have skyrocketed from one in seventeen to one in five. Or perhaps, like us, you're among the half a million British landlords who never meant to own a rental property but ended up doing so through moving jobs, partners or countries. Some inherited a property; others struggled to sell their home so decided to let it out instead. All these are accidental landlords.

We got married. Wanting a home that was new to both of us to start life together, we decided to let out the three-bedroom former council flat in leafy Southfields, southwest London, that Daniel had bought as a bachelor back in 2004. With a balcony so close to Wimbledon's tennis courts that you could hear the crowds roar at Andy Murray's triumphs, it turned out to be a great little earner that never stood empty. It helped us travel around the world, buy our first family house and invest in more property.

Friends who moved abroad started asking Daniel to look after their London homes, and so Swift Property, his specialist lettings agency, was born in 2010. It now has clients in thirteen countries across five continents, almost all of them accidental landlords with properties in London. They are people like John and Lily, who nervously let out their four-bedroom Edwardian terrace – complete with loft conversion, knocked-through living space and plantation shutters – after his job transferred to Switzerland.

Along the way, Swift has resolved hundreds of callouts. Besides its fair share of broken boilers, it has hired a security guard to shut down a neighbouring brothel and heated an entire flat to 60 degrees to kill bed bugs crawling up from the storey below. Once it even needed to rescue a pet python from a leak.

Meanwhile Martina, a property journalist at *The Sunday Times* newspaper, spent her days interviewing homeowners, investors and experts – winning awards for her accessible, engaging coverage.

In this book, we combine our experience and research to show you how to have peace of mind about your rental property. You will learn to let it hassle free, so you can spend your time settling into your new life, job or country – not fielding phone calls. You will be able to make the most of your asset, even using it as your first step to financial freedom.

After all, property has been Britain's best investment of the past 20 years. Much of this growth is caused by Britain's housing crisis. Every year since the 1980s, the country has been building up to 100,000 fewer homes than we need to keep up with the population. This has pushed up house prices so much that if food rose at the same rate, a chicken would now cost about £55, the charity Shelter says. As a result, private renting in England has more than doubled in the past decade from about 2 million households to 4.3 million. Despite the uncertainty brought by Britain's shock vote to leave the European Union, that underlying demand won't fall anytime soon. Brexit or no Brexit, the country still has a supply shortage of some 2 million homes, which will take at least a generation to build.

Economics aside, we think property is such a popular investment (read: obsession) because:

- It has intrinsic value. Unlike shares, which can fall to nothing simply because of market confidence, property values can only drop to a point. At the end of the day, we all need somewhere to live.
- Property is tangible. You can see it, touch it, build it, paint it. You can have your say on it, impress your friends with it and raise your children in it.
- It gives unusually high returns because you can use other people's money to invest in it. Try borrowing from the bank to buy shares!

- Property gives both income (rent) and capital growth (price rises). Cash produces only income (interest), while shares yield both types of return but their income (dividends) is far less certain.
- You can understand property. Not many people understand derivatives, as the financial crisis made abundantly clear.

However, property has its risks, too. There are more than 140 laws containing over 400 regulations on private letting in England. Legally, a tenancy means your home temporarily becomes your tenants' home. You are granting them rights over it that supersede your own. If you want to enter, you need to ask permission. To end the tenancy, you have to follow a set legal process – and if you got anything wrong along the way, the courts may not allow you to end the tenancy at all. Worse, you could face fines and even prison if you failed to keep the property safe. We're trying to scare you a bit because it is so important to get things right: good tenants, managed correctly.

On top of that, letting out your property is getting tougher in Britain. In the wake of Brexit, the property market could be jittery for years. Plus, landlords are becoming a political target of tax changes and ever tightening rules. To stop investors from outbidding first-time buyers for the limited housing supply, the government embarked on the Great Buy-to-let Bashing of 2015 (more of this later).

We think that making property less attractive as an investment has to be part of the plan to end the housing crisis. It will temper the wrong kind of demand, but it doesn't solve the real problem of supply. The only long-term solution is to build a lot more homes – and that will take a big political vision, which no recent government has shown. In the meantime, 'greedy' landlords make an easy scapegoat to deflect attention from the fact that decades of poor policy have caused far too few houses to be built, getting us into this pickle in the first place. We don't see this climate getting any better for landlords. It will likely get worse, making lettings that much harder.

This book will show you how to make a success of letting, whatever that looks like to you. It might be to start building a property portfolio, to get a monthly income or simply to get your home back in good nick. You might want to be involved in every detail, or just see the rent hit your account every month.

We cover all the questions most asked by homeowners in your shoes. In the course of our work, we have been surprised at the lack of resource for accidental landlords. There are lots of books on property investment, but those assume you are a would-be empire builder deliberately setting out to buy – not much help with the property you already own. Equally, there are several lettings handbooks aimed at landlords who know their EPC from their Section 21, but they are overly technical for beginners. It's a bit like starting to learn English by reading Shakespeare.

We can't walk you through the legal nitty-gritty of an eviction or the finite details of a capital gains calculation. We can neither share the formula to build an investment empire worth millions, nor tell you how to refurb your bathroom all by yourself (though Daniel is a super hero with a drain plunger, writes Martina). There are experts in all these areas who can help you. What we *can* do is to give you the unbiased, easy-to-understand overview that you need to achieve peace of mind as an accidental landlord.

Our aim is to be comprehensive – covering all the boxes you have to tick – yet practical, sharing the lessons Daniel has learnt in six years of looking after accidental landlords. And we've tried our darnedest to inject some fun into subjects that would otherwise put an insomniac to sleep. Among the boxes dotted throughout the text, you'll find some toe-curling stories to learn from. (Yup, the python and the brothel are in there, along with pigeon eggs in a tenant's bed, and they're all completely true. For reasons that will become obvious, all names have been changed.)

That said, this is not the sort of book you'd read from cover to cover on the beach. We have designed it as a reference guide to dip into along your landlord journey. To make it easy for you to find answers as you need them, we've broken down the lettings process into five Ps:

- **Plan.** The biggest mistake new landlords make – and how to avoid it. We help you to run your numbers, get the right financing and plan ahead to save thousands in tax. And we tell you the truth about agents.
- **Property.** All the practical steps to prepare your property for letting, peppered with tips on how to furnish, dress and market it. Plus, all the legal musts on being safe, green and licensed.
- **People.** From viewing to vetting, we explain how to find good tenants – and how to keep them, even when you raise the rent.
- **Paperwork.** Contracts, deposits, notices...The essentials to start and end a tenancy.
- **Practicals.** The 10 most common maintenance problems solved, plus 10 improvements that will pay off.

To make it even easier, we start off with a handy checklist of all the lettings steps you have to take. Then, once it's all going swimmingly, we look at how to buy more investment properties – and how to sell.

You may have started out as an accidental landlord, but to make a success of it, you need to be deliberate. Let's start with a plan.

Your all-in-one checklist

We've looked through piles of property books, dozens of reports and hundreds of web pages. Astoundingly, we couldn't find a single up-to-date checklist of all you need to do when you want to let out your home for the first time. So we decided to make one – and here it is. (Download an electronic version of this list for free at accidentallandlord.info/extras, so you can print it out and tick boxes to your heart's content.)

In the rest of this book, we will explore each point in more detail. To help you find that detail as you need it, we've included the five P sections that we have used across the book.

The list is chronological so you can use it to tick off each item while managing your own property, or to ensure your lettings agent does everything they should. If they slip up, the consequences can be serious – and you, not they, will be liable.

Plan

Four months before letting:

- ☐ Define your property goal, write your business plan and run your numbers. Based on that, decide whether you want to keep your property, refurbish it or sell
- ☐ Get consent to let from your mortgage provider, or switch to a buy-to-let mortgage
- ☐ Tell your buildings and contents insurers that you're planning to let out your home. Take out appropriate cover to kick in when letting starts
- ☐ Register for self-assessment tax with HMRC. From now on, you have to complete the property section as part of your annual return
- ☐ Get tax advice so you can structure your income to make the full use of all allowances. If you're married, transferring ownership now may save you thousands in tax

- [ ] If you're about to let out a leasehold flat, check your lease to see what obligations you have and get consent from the freeholder
- [ ] Decide whether you want to use a lettings agent. If so, appoint them; if not, decide whom you will ask to help run your property.

Property

Three months before letting:

- [ ] Do any necessary work to prepare your property for letting, such as repainting. If a big project is needed, decide whether you'll do it now or later
- [ ] Declutter your property and fix snags
- [ ] Furnish if necessary, and dress the interiors
- [ ] Have the property professionally photographed, get a floorplan and prepare the advert copy
- [ ] Set your asking rent, based on market rates
- [ ] Obtain an energy performance certificate (EPC) – a legal requirement before marketing. This lasts for 10 years. To see if your property already has one, check epcregister.com
- [ ] Apply to your council for a landlord licence if that's required in your area
- [ ] Apply to your council for a house in multiple occupation (HMO) licence – you may need one to let to three or more sharers. This usually takes two months to process.

Two months before each new tenancy:

- [ ] Advertise the property on Rightmove, Zoopla and/or OnTheMarket via your lettings agent or by using an online agent
- [ ] If the property has a gas supply, get an engineer on the Gas Safe Register to test it and issue a certificate. This is valid for a year

- [ ] Make sure an electrical safety check has been done in the last five years and check the electrical installation visually
- [ ] Install smoke and carbon monoxide detectors. All upholstered furniture must have fire-safety labels. For a share of a freehold flat, assess the fire risk in the common areas and fit a 30-minute fire door as the front door
- [ ] Assess the risk that the bacteria causing the potentially fatal Legionnaires' Disease could breed in the water system.

People

One month before letting:

- [ ] Host viewings, choose your tenants and negotiate the rent and tenancy terms
- [ ] Conduct thorough reference checks
- [ ] Check the identity documents of all adult tenants with them present to ensure they have a 'Right to Rent' in Britain.

Paperwork

Two weeks before letting:

- [ ] Draw up an assured shorthold tenancy agreement and get the tenants to sign it
- [ ] Register the deposit with one of three state-backed protection schemes within 30 days of receiving it
- [ ] Also within 30 days of receiving the deposit, issue the tenants with the prescribed information supplied by the protection scheme
- [ ] Give the tenants the latest version of the government's 'How To Rent' leaflet (gov.uk/government/publications/how-to-rent), as well as copies of the gas safety certificate and EPC. Ask them to acknowledge receipt by email or by signing and dating a paper copy of each document
- [ ] Write your house guide

- [ ] Transfer council tax and utility bills into the tenant's name. Set up a Royal Mail redirect for your own correspondence to prevent identity fraud
- [ ] Book a professional clean, including carpets, for at least 48 hours before the check-in. Check that all light bulbs work, that the chimneys are swept and the garden is tidy
- [ ] Hire an independent clerk to create a full written inventory with photos of the property's contents and condition.

On move-in day:

- [ ] Check in the tenants, hand them your house guide and the keys and talk them through what to do in an emergency. Ask them to sign agreement to the inventory report within seven days
- [ ] Check that the smoke and carbon monoxide detectors are working.

Practicals

During each tenancy:

- [ ] Inspect the property every six to nine months in appointments arranged at least 24 hours in advance
- [ ] Check the smoke and carbon monoxide detectors on each visit
- [ ] If any rent payments are late, email or call the tenants by noon of the day it is due
- [ ] Respond promptly to repair requests and update the tenants on the progress
- [ ] Renew the gas safety certificate annually and give the tenants a copy within 28 days of the test.

Paperwork (again)

Three months before each tenancy ends:

- [ ] If you're happy for the tenants to stay, decide if you want the tenancy to roll on into a periodic one, or to renew it for another fixed term

- ☐ Ask the tenants if they want to stay on. If you'd like to raise the rent, negotiate the increase now. Get them to sign the new contract, if there is one
- ☐ Do you want to end the tenancy? Then serve a Section 21 notice on your tenants at least two months before the end of the fixed term.

Six weeks before each tenancy ends:

- ☐ Email the tenants their check-in inventory plus a detailed list of how they should leave the property to avoid deductions.

At each tenancy's end:

- ☐ Get an independent clerk (theaiic.co.uk, apip.org.uk) to take meter readings and compare the property's contents and condition to the check-in inventory
- ☐ Ask the tenants to leave all the keys inside the property
- ☐ Negotiate any deposit deductions. Return the deposit to the tenants within 10 days of you both agreeing how much they'll get back. If you cannot agree, apply for resolution with the deposit protection scheme. Any amount in dispute stays in protection until you sort out the issue.

Note this list – and this book – is for lettings in England only. Some rules differ in Scotland, Wales and Northern Ireland; the National Landlords Association (landlords.org.uk) is a good place to check what applies locally.

One last thing: this list takes in the lettings process only – the subject of most of this book. If you want to do major works, buy or sell, read the final three chapters. For the sake of simplicity, we have not outlined these steps here.

Part 1
Plan

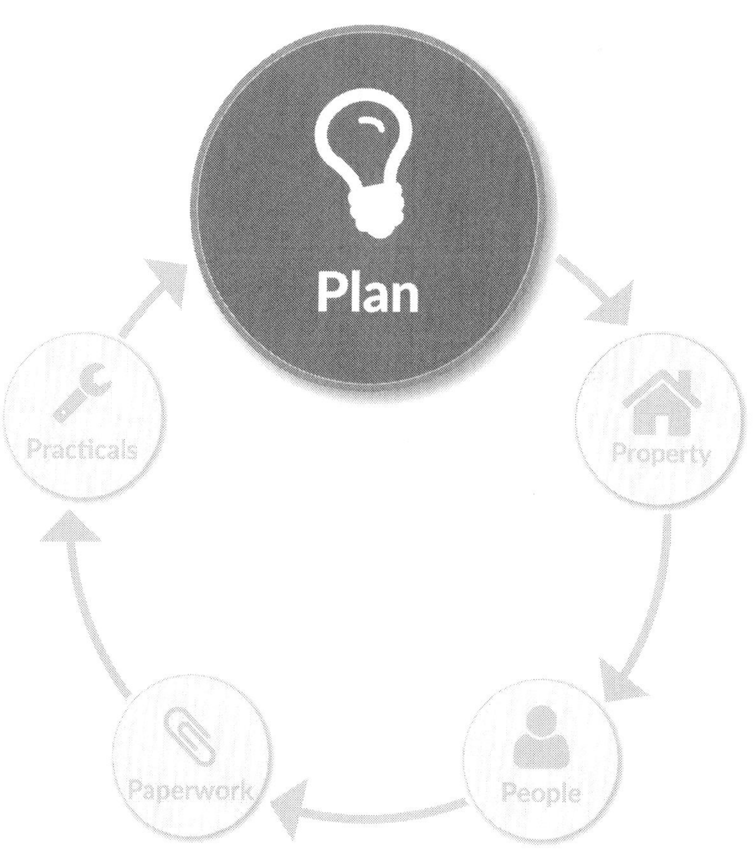

CHAPTER 1

How to avoid the No1 landlord mistake

In this chapter:

- **The big questions you need to ask yourself long before you call any agents**
- **How you can use your property as a step towards your dream lifestyle**
- **Six key points for a property business plan to get you where you want to be.**

What's the biggest mistake new landlords make? Martina has asked that question to many an expert, and here's the resounding answer: beginners don't think of their property as a business. For accidental landlords who see their property as their home, the shift is even harder. But to make a success of letting out your property, that shift is essential.

Your rental property is probably one of your largest financial assets. Astoundingly, though, a representative survey of 500 buy-to-let owners by the investment franchise Platinum Property Partners found that 93% of landlords have no five-year plan whatsoever for their properties.

In this section we help you change your mindset by thinking about your product, target audience and competition. That will enable you to make clear-headed decisions. What's more, you can then use your property as a stepping-stone to the lifestyle you really want.

Before you draw up your business plan, though, you need to think about your goal. Why? Your plan is your map; your goal is your destination. If you don't know where you're going, you may create a map that takes you to the wrong place. Do you want to start a new career? Retire with a nest egg? Spend life in a hammock? Your plan will look quite different for each of those goals. One rental property won't get you there, but it can become a big step towards that goal if you act wisely.

At this point, you may be saying, 'I didn't choose to be a landlord; it sort of chose me. Should I really bother with these airy-fairy questions? I'm more worried about having my home looked after – what if my garden dies or squatters move in? And where on earth do I find a decent agent?'

We'll get to all that, but thinking about the bigger picture first will open your eyes to new lifestyle possibilities. It will also help you make better decisions on the smaller stuff, such as which tenants to accept or whether you should revamp the kitchen. Without a goal, you may end up not only wasting money on unnecessary works but also wasting the opportunity to build the life you desire.

Income spinner traded for growth giver

Remember our ex-council flat near Wimbledon's tennis courts? It was the scene of the first (and only) candlelit dinner that Daniel cooked in our dating days. Once we were married and renting it out, it brought in more than £1,000 a month in profit – paying our bills as Daniel launched Swift property and funding our adventures from Patagonian glaciers to private islands in the Med. Yet 10 years on, despite the fond memories and tidy income, we sold it. Why? It didn't meet our goal anymore.

With a second baby on the way, we needed a plan to afford a bigger London house by the time the kids outgrew their shared bedroom.

A rental property poised for capital growth – not income – would help fund the leap up the ladder. After a lot of research, we reinvested our Wimbledon gains in a period flat in Maida Hill, an undervalued pocket on the northwestern fringe of central London. The figures still stacked up: it yielded £400 a month in profit. But, crucially for our goal, its value also rose by nearly £100,000 a year – an annual growth rate of 16%, compared to 6.7% for the ex-council flat.

Define your property goal

Long before you pick up the phone to any lettings agents, you need to ask yourself some big questions: what is my dream lifestyle? How much money do I need from my property to get there? And by when do I want to achieve it?

A clear goal has three elements. It is:

1. **Meaningful.** To motivate you to action, your goal should state your big 'why'. For example, you might want to build up a nest egg for retirement far into the future, or you're starting a business and you need some money in the bank every month. Our 'why' was to buy a London house big enough to swing two kids in.
2. **Specific.** If your goal is too vague, you won't know when you've achieved it – this is where 'I want to live comfortably' falls short. You need to quantify how much you want to earn.
3. **Timed.** Deadlines make all the difference. Are you saving to help your children on to the property ladder in a decade's time, or to pay their school fees from next year? Your approach for each will be poles apart, as we'll see in a moment.

In short, 'I want a family house' is a dream; 'I want £100,000 in equity from my rental flat to buy a bigger family house in three years' time' is a goal.

Do you need income or growth target?

Your goal will determine whether you need to focus on rental income (for money in the bank every month) or long-term price growth (for a lump sum one day).

If you are buying your first property, you can choose one suited to your goals. But as an accidental landlord, you already have a property – and it might not give you what you really want. Going through the goal exercise will help you work out your next moves: should you keep it, sell it, improve it or remortgage to buy another just like it?

In the next chapter, we will look at how to measure income and growth, so you can evaluate how your property performs. For now, though, we want you to start thinking how you can use it as a first step to set your course in any number of ways. Here are a few examples to inspire you:

Executive parent.

'I want to pay my children's school fees and/or boost my income while I build up my new business.'

Income or growth? Income – enough monthly rental profit to cover the school fees and/or shortfall in the family budget.

Ideal property. High cash flow with tenancy management outsourced, such as an ex-council flat or older new build in outer London, or small houses within a mile's commute of city centres like Liverpool or Leeds.

Next steps. Renting out what used to be your starter home? This might be a good fit as your target tenant will be yourself a few years younger. A minor spruce-up might be all that's needed, but if those school fees are high, you could consider remortgaging down the line to buy another income spinner.

Grandlord.

'I'm retired and want to add to my pension income.'

Income or growth? Mainly rental income, but it should be secure with low maintenance to limit stress. To work out your profit target, calculate your average monthly spend, add a 30% buffer and then deduct your current income.

Ideal property. A high-quality, low-maintenance home with strong rental demand, for example city-centre flats in Birmingham or Manchester.

Next steps. If you've downsized and are now letting out your former family home, you might want to sell this and buy something that would let more easily and require less maintenance. Also, consider longer tenancies for extra security.

Forward planner.

'I want to create a nest egg for my children and/or build up extra income to maintain my lifestyle when I retire one day.'

Income or growth? Long-term price growth, but with enough income to cover your costs. Your growth target is whichever big lump sum you want to cash in on far into the future. Time is on your side, so you can afford to take more risks.

Ideal property. A wow property in an established area that will rise in value, such as central London, Cambridge or Solihull.

Next steps. Make sure the rent covers your costs in the meantime and set aside cash reserves. Avoid having too much debt on the property, which would push up your monthly costs. If the place then sits empty, you could be forced to sell your nest egg.

Second-stepper.

'I can't yet afford my forever home, so need a leg up.'

Income or growth? Growth – and capital preservation. To calculate your growth target, deduct the deposit that you'll need for your dream home from your current savings and equity. You can't afford to lose any money, so avoid risk.

Ideal property. A period property (older than 100 years) on the edge of an attractive area, where prices are likely to rise because of gentrification. Forthcoming transport links or big regeneration projects nearby will have the same effect.

Next steps. Rather than just relying on market growth, work out if you can add value with a makeover or extension. You could also try solving a legal problem such as extending a short lease or getting planning permission for works.

Fear not, we won't tell you to now silently recite your vision until the universe comes into alignment. We won't even ask you to stick it on your bathroom mirror. But think about your goal and write it down, so you can use it to guide your decisions about your property.

Create your business plan

Now that you know where you want to go, you can map out how to get there. This involves creating a business plan. After all, property is a business that can benefit from the same principles as any other type of business.

Think about:

1. **Your product.** What are your property's strengths and weaknesses?
2. **Your target audience.** Who is your ideal tenant? Would your property attract them? How much demand is there in your area from such tenants?
3. **Your competition.** How many similar properties to yours are nearby? How does yours compare?
4. **Your exit strategy.** How long do you want to keep your property? Do you intend to sell it, return to it or keep it and buy more?
5. **Your numbers.** What should you budget for? Do your figures stack up?

6. **Your team.** Who will let and manage your property: yourself or an agent? If you intend to self-manage, do you want to outsource anything, such as repairs?

In the rest of this chapter, we'll explore the first four points. Running your numbers and choosing your management team are more complex subjects, so we will cover those separately over the next few chapters.

Analyse your product

Be honest about your property's strengths and weaknesses. You might not have bought it with renting in mind, so some factors could make it harder to let, for example, if it's far from public transport or near a large council estate. Though you can't change its location, you can find ways to work around it. You can also change its presentation if, say, it's filled with too many personal items or looking a tad tired (more of this later).

Rugby player scores despite location blight

Chris was keen to buy his first property and settled for a small terraced house near a large housing estate and a local nightclub. When he got married and moved abroad to play professional rugby, he let out his home through Swift. The council estate, it turned out, put off some would-be tenants. However, by taking the following steps, Chris ensured that his house never sat empty:

- He was realistic on the type of tenants he would attract. A young family who worried about safety didn't take it, but a young couple and their brother – all new to the country – liked that they could get more space for less money

- During viewings, all the facts were on hand to answer questions upfront. The nightclub, for example, was going to be turned into housing – improving the area
- Chris was flexible on the deposit, accepting a deposit paid by a council scheme on the tenants' behalf
- He was accommodating with furniture, buying a bed for certain tenants, then getting rid of a desk for the next ones
- He allowed tenants to paint the house inside, as long as they returned it to its original colours afterwards.

Identify your target audience

Which type of tenant is your property likely to attract? Who would want to live in this location, with these nearby facilities (for example, transport, schools or parks), in a property of this size, style and layout?

It helps to profile your target audience so you can gear your property towards their needs. For instance, if you would like to let to a family but your property is a second-floor flat with no lift, the stairs will put off anyone with a buggy. It would be wiser to aim for young professionals and kit out the flat with simple, modern furniture. This will make your place stand out from similar properties nearby.

Knowing your market will also help you decide which upgrades to make (new kitchen or just a repaint?), as well as how to market and dress the property.

Plus, you will be more prepared for any problems common to your type of tenant. For example, you can educate young tenants from the start that they have to put rinse aid in the dishwasher instead of having to fix said dishwasher down the line.

Below is a table with a (very generalised) list of tenant types and what they want. In Chapter 10 'The dos and don'ts for six tenant types' we'll look at most of these groups in more detail.

TENANT TYPE	NEEDS	BENEFITS	WATCH OUT
Students	▸ Three+ bedrooms (even if small) ▸ Opportunity to fit in many people to save costs ▸ Walking distance or with good transport links to campus ▸ In student area near shops and nightlife ▸ Fully furnished, but cheap and easy to replace ▸ All bills and broadband included ▸ Secure bike storage is a big plus	▸ Predictable tenant changeover at end of academic year ▸ Students pay no council tax, so rent can be higher than for professionals ▸ Parents often act as guarantors ▸ Sometimes pay six months' rent upfront	▸ Parties, careless behaviour and mess ▸ More wear and tear means higher maintenance costs ▸ Need to educate them to look after a property ▸ Turn lounges into bedrooms, making it harder to rent to non-students afterwards ▸ You may need a licence for a house in multiple occupation (HMO) ▸ Your mortgage choices are limited
Newly-qualified professionals	▸ One+ bedrooms ▸ Reasonable rent ▸ No more than 10 minutes' walk to good transport ▸ Fully furnished (Ikea will do just fine)	▸ Responsible	▸ Often need to be educated on their responsibilities

TENANT TYPE	NEEDS	BENEFITS	WATCH OUT
Professional couple 25+	▸ One+ bedrooms ▸ A smart property ▸ No more than 10 minutes' walk to good transport ▸ Parking space ▸ Up-to-date furniture but may want to buy their own	▸ Sufficient income to cover the rent easily	▸ Can be demanding with an entitlement mentality ▸ Can be difficult to manage fallout if they split up ▸ Usually don't stay too long – often looking to buy
Professional single(s) 30+	▸ One+ bedrooms. Sharers want equal-sized bedrooms and two bathrooms ▸ A smart property ▸ No more than 10 minutes' walk to good transport ▸ Parking space ▸ Midrange furniture but they may have their own ▸ Privacy and security can be important ▸ Outside space a nice-to-have	▸ Can make the best tenants overall. Respectful and usually look after the property well	▸ Partner moving in without consent ▸ If letting to three or more sharers, you may need an HMO licence, which also limits mortgage choices

TENANT TYPE	NEEDS	BENEFITS	WATCH OUT
New to Britain	▸ Not particularly fussy about the property or location ▸ Often need to move quickly ▸ Need some flexibility on reference checks	▸ Can be great tenants, often very respectful of the property ▸ Can often move in at short notice	▸ May fail reference checks due to a lack of UK credit history ▸ Cultural differences may mean they overcrowd the property or don't understand tenant responsibilities
Housing benefit	▸ Two+ bedrooms ▸ May have own furniture to bring ▸ Garden (if they have children) ▸ Near local shop and well-run school	▸ Can be lucrative for cheaper properties that still rent at the government rate for the whole area ▸ Huge demand due to shortage of social rent properties ▸ Families can be stable long-term tenants	▸ Can default as benefit is paid to tenant, not landlord ▸ Some can't afford a deposit ▸ Can cause more wear and tear ▸ Can disappear overnight ▸ Your mortgage choices are limited

TENANT TYPE	NEEDS	BENEFITS	WATCH OUT
Families	▸ Two+ bedrooms ▸ Garden ▸ Good park nearby ▸ Catchment area for good schools ▸ Storage for buggies and scooters ▸ No (or few) stairs to front door ▸ Unfurnished as they usually have their own furniture ▸ Parking space	▸ Very stable; usually stay long term for schools	▸ Young children or pets can cause damage

Assess your competition

How many properties similar to yours are up for rent nearby? Knowing how unique your property is for the area will help you establish how best to differentiate and market it. For example, in large new build developments a lot of flats with similar finishes and floorplans can hit the rental market at the same time – driving down rents. If you're buying, steer clear for this reason. But if you already own such a flat, ensure that you furnish and present it so it stands out from the crowd. Plus, in this scenario it's particularly important to get your pricing levels just right.

Flowers knock out new build competition

When Bruno bought his canal-side flat in Northolt, west London, it was one of the first to be completed in its new build development. Eight years on, he and Sally, his new wife, left the country to study in America and put the two-bedroom flat up for rent. By now, the development had become vast, with dozens of similar flats on the rental market.

However, because Bruno chose his flat right at the start of the development, it had one thing going for it: its garden right beside the canal. Bruno and Sally worked hard to make their garden look its best, planting bright flowers and waiting until they were in full bloom before having it professionally photographed. They also included their stylish leather sofa and decluttered the flat before viewings. It paid off: it let above market rate and never stood empty.

Keep your exit strategy in mind

What is your long-term plan with your property? Do you want to hold it? Sell it? Return to it? Your answer will steer your decisions.

If you're planning to sell in the next few years, it makes sense to avoid any major upgrades unless they will raise the sale price. Instead, you will just keep the property ticking over. Ideally you want to secure a top rent and not be too fussy about the tenant type. Importantly, you will structure tenancy agreements so that you can give notice when you need to.

However, if you intend to hold your property for many years, it's much more critical to get the type of tenant who will look after it and ideally stay longer term. This may mean accepting a slightly lower rent. In the long run, it's usually more cost effective to tackle any maintenance problems proactively before they become major issues.

Likewise, whether or not you plan to return to your property will determine your choice of finishes: do you go for personal preference or durability and wide appeal? You can justify those hand-painted Moroccan bathroom tiles if it's going to be your domain again; if not, your tenants might be happier with simple white porcelain.

Sale chills boiler plans

Jenny and David had an inefficient old back boiler in their 1930s house, which landed their tenants with astronomical energy bills. The unhappy tenants pushed for an efficient new combi-boiler and the landlords got a number of quotes. Yet at the same time the landlords decided to sell the house, so they then opted to keep the existing boiler but give a goodwill contribution towards the tenants' energy costs. A new boiler would have cost them around £5,000, but wouldn't have increased their sale price.

You now know how to avoid the biggest mistake new landlords make – shift from seeing your property as your home to seeing it as a business. By taking into account your product, target audience, competition and exit strategy, you are well on your way to creating a business plan – putting you a step ahead of more than half of landlords who lack one altogether.

Crucially, though, you still need to do your sums and decide who will manage your property. Over the rest of the 'Plan' section, we will walk you through these aspects, starting with those all-important numbers (even if you find spreadsheets about as confusing as what women see in Russell Brand).

CHAPTER 2

Run your numbers

PLAN

In this chapter:

- **The investment principles of income, growth and leverage in plain English**
- **How to measure your property's performance through yield and more**
- **What to budget for and how to estimate your rent accurately.**

You are now in the buy-to-let business. You might be an accidental landlord, but you can't run your property in an accidental way. Three in ten landlords with a single property only break even or make a loss, according to the National Landlords Association. How can you ensure that you'll be among those who make a healthy profit?

A key part of the plan discussed in the previous chapter is to do your sums. Start with a financial audit: what is your property's market value? What would it rent for? What are your outstanding mortgage and monthly payments?

Next you need to measure how your home performs as an investment. Before we jump into the maths to help you do that, we'll first race through the basics of property economics: leverage, income and growth. Finally we'll have a good old sit-down with a spreadsheet to make sure your budget includes everything it should.

By the end of this chapter, you'll be able to decide what you want to do with your property. If it's a B league player, you can start thinking about a medium-term plan to sell it and buy something else. Should it be a star performer, you can plan ahead to perhaps take out equity and use it to buy another – or, at the very least, have peace of mind that the figures do stack up.

Property economics 101: basic investment principles

Leverage

Why is property such a good thing to invest in? The answer lies in leverage, also called gearing. As the word suggests, it acts like a lever: if you apply a small force (your deposit) to a lever (your mortgage), it amplifies the effect (your return).

In a rising market, this catapults what would have been ordinary returns into phenomenal ones. Though the cost of your property is not all yours – the bank funds the rest of it – you get all the gains (or losses, as shown in the panel below, so beware).

The double-edged sword of leverage

Here's how leverage works (and for the sake of simplicity, we'll leave out fees and taxes). Three friends each buy a £100,000 flat and sell them five years on for £150,000 a pop – a £50,000 gain for all three. For Cash-rich Charlie, who bought his flat outright, this means a respectable 50% return. Mortgaged Moira, who put down a £25,000 deposit, gets a hefty 200% return. But Leveraged Luke, whose deposit was only £10,000, walks away with a whopping 500% return.

However, leverage is a double-edged sword. Let's say a recession hits after a year, all three friends lose their jobs and have to sell their flats to get by – but now the property values have dipped to £80,000. Charlie loses 20% of the money he put in, but has £80,000 to live on. Once Moira has paid back her mortgage, she has only £5,000 left – having lost 80% of her £25,000 deposit.

Poor Luke, though, is worst off: an £80,000 sale price is not enough to repay his £90,000 loan. He is stuck in negative equity, with his money trapped in the flat until its price rises. If his tenant now also loses her job and stops paying rent, Luke could fall behind on his mortgage payments and have his flat repossessed – losing 100% of his money and his ability to get credit in the future.

Put simply, leverage means you can expose yourself to more capital growth. Instead of buying one flat outright, Cash-rich Charlie could use his £100,000 for four 25% deposits. In our five-year scenario above, that would bag him £200,000 – *four times as much profit for the same cash input.*

But leverage brings two dangers: the risk of losing big if the market falls, as illustrated above, and the cost of eating into your cash flow. The more you borrow, the more interest you have to pay. That makes it harder to make a monthly profit from your rent – especially if you are a higher-rate taxpayer, under new changes.

This is also why it's dangerous to over-leverage: if interest rates rise – and they will – you could end up having to pay into your property every month. If you then can't afford that and have to sell, but at the same time prices plummet so far that you can't clear your mortgage, you could face bankruptcy.

To hedge against this, make sure your cash flow can weather short-term storms such as empty periods, unexpected repair bills or interest rate rises. As long as you can hold out through the downturns, your property is likely to rise in value over time. Since the start of Nationwide's market index in 1953, British prices have risen 8% a year on average, despite cyclical dips along the way.

Income versus growth

Besides leverage, the second reason property is a great asset is that it combines two forms of return: long-term capital growth *and* regular income (rent). Cash gives you income alone (interest); shares can give you capital growth and only sporadic income (dividends).

As discussed in the previous chapter, your property goal might mean that you prioritise income or growth, but both are important. You see, growth is a gamble: even though the average British house price has doubled every nine years, an average is not an average for all. At the time of writing – eight years on from the financial crisis – prices in vibrant cities such as Liverpool and Glasgow are still below their 2008 peak, according to Hometrack's cities index. Yes, you can do a refurb to add value, but you have little control over your area's price growth (or lack of it). This is why capital growth should be a long-term target, not something you rely on over a two- or three-year period.

Income, on the other hand, is much more of a sure thing. If you clear £500 in monthly rental profit, that's £500 dropping into your bank account every month, crunch or no crunch. There could be interest rate rises, gaps between tenants or a big maintenance bill, but you can budget for all that and, in the long run, depend on your £500.

So, if the rent falls short of your mortgage payment and you have to fork out every month, think twice about keeping your property just to gamble on growth. In the giddy years before the crunch, some landlords didn't even put tenants into their properties – it was less bother to shell out themselves while watching prices soar. As they found out, you'll face a double whammy if prices drop.

Could you have it all, then – high income *and* high growth? Probably not, especially if you are talking about a home that you bought to live in, rather than as a cleverly chosen investment. And even cleverly chosen buy-to-lets usually involve a trade-off between income and growth: a stucco-fronted flat in central

London is the classic growth buy, but has low rental yields because it's so expensive in the first place. Meanwhile a run-down terrace in, say, Leeds could rent well despite its low price – which means good income but poor price growth prospects.

The wisest approach is to balance income and growth: rent that not only covers your costs but leaves you with an ample buffer, combined with long-term uplift from gentrification and regeneration in your area. Everything in moderation, as they say. In short:

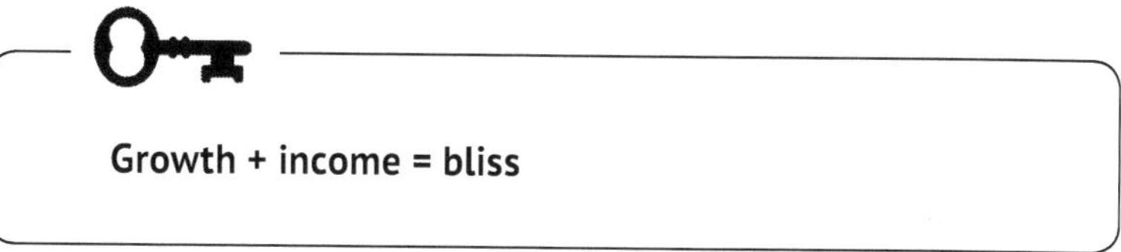

Property maths 101: how to measure success

How, then, do you measure success in income and growth? Before we dive into the calculations, a quick note: apart from stamp duty, tax is not included here. Because tax is so specific to your individual circumstances, it's impossible to account for it in these generic formulae.

Now, let's start with how you evaluate income.

Measuring income

There are three simple ways to measure income success, each useful in a different setting:

Gross yield

If someone talks about 'yield' without saying which type, they usually mean gross yield. This is the yield before you've taken any costs into account:

What is a good yield? As a rough rule of thumb, once you've accounted for costs, you'll struggle to break even on a gross yield under 4%. For a better income, look for a gross yield of 7%–9%.

You'll hear the term 'yield' thrown around a lot if you're looking at buy-to-lets. Be aware, though, that many people misunderstand what it means, or even deliberately try to mislead you with glossy yields. Do your own sums.

When it's useful. As a rough-and-ready shortcut to compare properties that are likely to have similar running costs, like two modern flats.

Net yield

To be more precise, factor in your running costs. Net yield takes into account mortgage interest, agent fees, repairs, service charges, insurance and loss of income when the property is empty – all of which we'll cover in more detail later. If a seller quotes you a net yield, do check what they include so you can compare like with like.

When it's useful. To compare properties that have different running costs – a flat and a house, say, as long as you can accurately estimate the expenses.

Return on investment (ROI)

In the net yield calculation above, 2% sounds like a paltry return. Why bother with tenants and tradesmen if you can just as well stash your cash in a savings account? Crucially, though, the cash wasn't all your own – you borrowed much of it from the bank. Enter the power of leverage.

If you have a mortgage, calculate the yield based not on the purchase price, but on how much of your own money you invested:

Ta da! Suddenly all the bother seems worth it.

To get the whole picture, under 'cash invested' add all purchase costs to your deposit: stamp duty, surveys, legal and mortgage fees.

When it's useful. To see how hard your money is working not just compared to other properties, but also to other asset classes. ROI helps you decide whether to invest in property, stocks or cash.

Measuring growth

When you're buying a new property, stick to the three income calculations above to compare options. Even if you're buying with growth in mind, there's no way to predict what *future* growth will be. The only certainty is that it will differ from what you expect.

However, if you are deciding whether to sell or keep letting out your existing home, you can take its *past capital growth* into account:

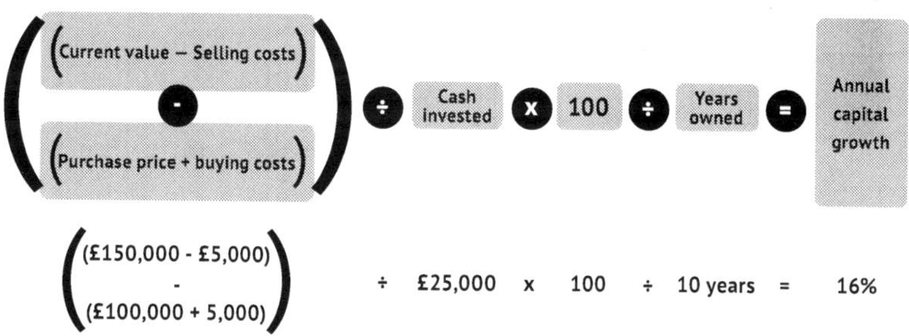

You can then use this annual capital growth to work out your total property return:

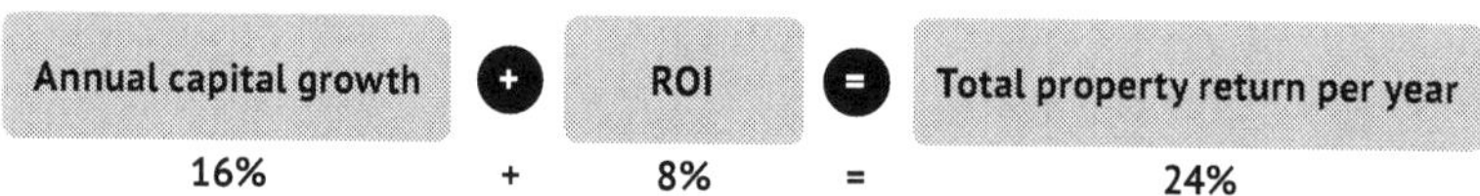

Pffft, try to beat that with a savings account. Yet before you crack open the champagne to celebrate your paper profit, bear in mind that it's just that until you actually sell. Before then, its increase in value is pure theory; ultimately it will be worth what a buyer pays for it.

Property accounting 101: what to budget for

Of course, the answers to your new calculations are only as good as the data you put in. Whether you're gauging your home's performance as an investment or hunting for your first buy-to-let, you need to pinpoint:

- **Buying costs**
- **Rent.** Pair this with the buying costs to work out the gross yield
- **Running costs.** Deduct this from the rent to calculate your net yield or ROI.

Buying costs

To help beginners buying an investment property, we include typical amounts to budget for:

- **The property itself.** Your biggest cost by far. To buy with a buy-to-let mortgage, you'll need a deposit of at least 25% (more about that in the next chapter). Your purchase price will of course be clear if you've already paid it, but it's not that simple if you're looking to buy. The asking price is not the same as the property's actual market value – the price you *should* pay. We tell you how to work out what a property's really worth in the chapter on buying near the end of this book.
- **Stamp duty.** As part of the Great Buy-to-let Bashing of 2015, which we mentioned in the introduction, our esteemed chancellor walloped investors with an extra 3% stamp duty on buy-to-lets. Work out what you'd pay (or gloat about what you've saved under the old regime) with the handy calculator at thesundaytimes.co.uk/stampduty.

- **Legal fees.** Solicitors' service levels vary, to put it politely. This is not a corner worth cutting: snail-paced conveyancing can lose you a deal, not to mention cost you even more dearly if your solicitor misses something nasty. Avoid any websites like supercheapsolitors.com; budget £750–£2,000 including legal searches.
- **Surveys.** Your mortgage provider will expect you to pay for a simple valuation (£300–£400) to check the property is worth its price. You can also do your own survey to check the building's structure. A Home Buyer Report (£350–£950) is enough in most cases; do a full Building Survey (£500–£1,300) if the property is listed, old or of non-standard construction.
- **Finance fees.** There are mortgage arrangement fees (as much as 3% of the loan), booking fees (£100–£200), broker fees (£0–£500), for-the-fun-of-it fees...
- **Works.** It's usually wise to set aside a few hundred pounds for fixing snags and redecorating. Before you do any bigger refurbs, read Chapter 16 'Make the improvements that matter'.
- **Furniture** – if you're letting your property furnished, that is. With clever buys, you can furnish a two-bedroom flat to a high standard for under £2,000.
- **Search agent fees** if you've used your own buying agent to find the property (2%–3.5% of purchase price).

Accurate rent estimate

Let's get one thing straight: *the market, not the landlord, dictates the rent.* Forget about asking £100 a month more just because your mortgage rate is up. Laid-back tenants who have stayed on for years without a rent rise *might* oblige, but the rest will take their business elsewhere. Beware, too, of letting agents who butter you up with inflated rents to win the business. Your property will simply languish empty until you drop the price. There is too much competition out there for you to try your luck.

However, with a bit of research you can estimate the monthly rent you'll achieve to within £50:

- **Find comparables online.** On Rightmove or Zoopla, look for properties to rent nearby of the same size and quality. Search for the same number of bedrooms as your property within ¼ mile of its postcode, sort in price order and click into the results to see how they compare with yours. Also tick the box to view 'let agreed' properties, which will show you how long they were advertised. If you come up blank, first look at homes with one more or one less bedroom nearby, then widen your search radius. This should give you an idea of the price range. Bear in mind, though, that these are all asking rents, not achieved rents; unfortunately, there is no nationwide database of past rents.
- **Call local agents.** Ask the agents who advertised comparable properties what they ended up letting for. You can also ask them to send you details of similar properties they have let recently.
- **London lettings differ.** In central London, rents depend more on square footage than the number of bedrooms. This is the only area with a database of past rents: good agents here have access to the LonRes network that includes up-to-the-minute lettings figures.
- **Be honest with yourself.** We all think our children are the prettiest, but being blind to your property's faults will cost you.
- **Listen to your agent.** If you trust your agent, take their advice.
- **Act when you need to.** No viewings after two weeks? Then the rent is too high. Don't wait for your agent to contact you but lower it decisively – not just by £10.

This valuation process will also show you whether the property will rent at all. You'll be able to gauge the local demand and how much competition there is. The same sort of quirks that put off buyers (weird layouts, poky rooms) will limit its appeal to tenants. If it's going to be too tough to let out, and you can't do anything to change that, it might be time to say goodbye.

Market, not mortgage, sets the rent

Jack and Karen had a hefty mortgage to pay on their swish one-bedroom flat in Kingston, southwest London. So when they decided to travel around the world, they put the flat up for rent at £1,350 a month – £50 above the highest market rate advised by their lettings agent. After one initial viewing, things went quiet for three weeks. No interest whatsoever. On their agent's advice, they lowered the price to the going rate of £1,275, and, hey presto, three viewings took place the next day. Two of the viewers offered and the deal was done with the more suitable tenant. Because the couple acted in time, they had no void period, which would have cost them almost £300 a week.

Running costs

Now, you can try and budget for every last key, stamp and phone call, but the only certainty about monthly expenses is that you'll be wrong. We try to be wrong in the right direction, with broad but pessimistic estimates of:

- **Mortgage repayments.** If you have a mortgage, this will almost always be your biggest cost. To make sure you can afford it if interest rates rise, stress test for a 7% repayment rate. (The historical UK base rate averages 5%, with typical variable-rate mortgages at 2% above that.)
- **Maintenance.** You never know when the boiler will go belly up or the shower sprout a leak. Costs are hard to predict and vary hugely by property type. You can use 5–10% of the annual rent as a starting point.
- **Service charges and ground rent.** You'll have to pay these annually for a flat or leasehold property. Costs vary depending

on the building's style and age, number of flats, state of repair and facilities. Stucco facades, lifts or underground parking all mean you'll cough up more.

- **Agent fees.** If you use an agent to let and/or manage your property, this will set you back 7–20% of the rent.
- **Insurance.** You'll need landlord buildings insurance as a minimum, or you could be left with nothing but a mortgage to pay if your place burns down. (See the next chapter for other insurance you might want.)
- **Empty periods,** also known as 'voids'. Factor in the cost of lost rent when your property stands empty between tenancies or to do works. Some landlords assume this will not happen, but it's prudent to budget for at least 1–2 months of lost rent a year.
- **Utility bills.** Only if you pay them, for example when you rent out your property by room.

No, we haven't forgotten that tax is a cost. You will be taxed on all property income less allowable expenses. However, because tax varies so much depending on your circumstances, we will deal with it in detail in Chapter 4 'Think ahead to save a fortune in tax'.

Now that your spreadsheet is free of holes (and worthy of an investment geek badge), you can set aside reserves for any shortfalls. You know whether or not your property is a star investment, so you can plan ahead to sell, buy more or remortgage – which brings us to the subject of the next chapter.

CHAPTER 3

Switch to the right mortgage and insurance

PLAN

In this chapter

- **Why you can't stay on your residential mortgage or normal insurance**
- **How to choose a buy-to-let mortgage – and how much you can borrow**
- **Do you really need insurance? And if so, which cover?**

Seldom has there been a more riveting topic than mortgages and insurance. (Yawn.) But before you glaze over, this chapter can mean the difference between losing and keeping your home.

You might think that, as long as you pay your residential mortgage, your lender won't notice or care if you start letting out your home, right?

Wrong.

Strictly speaking, you would be committing mortgage fraud. Though less serious than taking out a mortgage under false pretences, this would still breach the contract that you signed with your lender, in which you have promised to live in the property and not let it out without their consent. Worst case, your lender can call in your loan and demand that you immediately pay it off in full (see anecdote). They can also fine you, raise your rate – possibly more than they would have if you'd come clean – or put a black mark on your credit record.

In areas where councils require landlords to have a licence, you need to disclose your mortgage details on the application form. The councils then write to the lender to tell them about your licence application. This has caught out increasing numbers of accidental landlords with the wrong loans. Some lenders also check on the electoral register, social media and lettings adverts to see whether properties have been put up for rent. You have been warned.

It's even more serious when it comes to insurance. *Your buildings insurance is likely to be invalid if you let out your home without telling your provider.* If your house then burns down, you won't get a penny but will still have to pay back your mortgage.

We'll walk you through your alternatives for both mortgages and insurance. You'll learn how much you can borrow, what lenders require and which insurance you really need. Even if you're buying your first buy-to-let property rather than letting out the place where you used to live, most of this chapter will be just as useful to you.

'Lenders do care – and do call in loans'

Specialist brokers report a rise in mortgages that are revoked when landlords are on the wrong product. 'Lenders most definitely do care and do take action,' says Lisa Orme, managing director of Keys Mortgages, who has picked up the pieces in several such cases. One client, who let out her home without permission, was given three months to sell or pay off her loan in full – without any negotiation.

Another, who had numerous mortgages with the same lender, used a single-tenancy mortgage for a property that was actually let by room to sharers on separate contracts. When the landlord applied to remortgage, a valuer inspected the place and reported the breach. The lender called in all the loans – even the legitimate ones – and charged redemption penalties on the lot.

'A third client got his residential lender's consent to let his home to students. Months later, the council brought in new rules that required the landlord to get an additional licence for a house in multiple occupation. However, because any licensing would breach the mortgage terms, the lender then gave the client 28 days to redeem the mortgage or get rid of the licence by getting rid of the tenants. He managed to negotiate a six-month hiatus to change loans.

Why you can't keep your old mortgage

So, if you have a residential mortgage on the property you're about to let out, what are your options? You can:

- Ask your current lender for **consent to let**
- Take out a new **buy-to-let mortgage.**

Before we look at these options in more detail, another warning: your mortgage is a big deal. You don't want to pick one based on what some guy in a book tells you. If you take one bit of advice from this guy (and girl), though, make it that: speak to a good mortgage broker. Not just any broker – definitely not the one at your bank, who can only offer you loans from their company's range. And probably not the one at your estate agent, as they're there to make extra money for the branch. Make sure it's an independent broker who covers the whole of the market. Choose a buy-to-let (rather than residential) specialist – and all the better if they own a buy-to-let themselves as they'll know which questions to ask.

Consent to let

If you are letting out your home for year or two, for example while working abroad, your best option is to apply to your current mortgage provider for 'consent to let'. Whether they'll give you consent, for what period and at what cost all depends on the lender. Some will load your interest rate by 1%; almost all will charge an admin fee, for example £100.

If your lender refuses consent to let and tries to force you on to one of its own buy-to-let mortgages, shop around first as you might get a better buy-to-let deal elsewhere.

Why do lenders get tetchy about this? They say they take on more risk if you let out the property (even though there are fewer defaults on buy-to-let mortgages than on residential ones). That's rich coming from banks whose greed got us all into a pickle in the first place. Yet fair or not, they are within their rights to require that you stick to your deal with them.

Buy-to-let mortgages

For longer lettings, you'll need to switch to a buy-to-let mortgage. Coined as a world first by Britain in 1996, these loans are based on what your property would let for, instead of – as for residential mortgages – what you earn.

Fees can be steep (£12,000, anyone?); rates and deposits are higher than for residential homes. On the upside, most are interest-only, which keeps your monthly repayments down.

Interest only or capital repayment?

As a homeowner, you'll be used to a capital repayment mortgage, in which you repay a bit of the loan every month until you own your house outright. But that's usually not the best for buy-to-let. Why?

An interest-only mortgage gives you better cash flow, lowering the risk that the rent won't cover your monthly costs, as we've seen when we looked at leverage. Plus, after an initial lock-out period, you will normally have the option to pay back chunks of capital at will – giving you the best of both worlds.

In the long term, inflation erodes what you need to repay anyway: over the course of a 25-year interest-only mortgage term, your property's value will rise but the loan amount stays the same.

However, think about your circumstances. If you want to return to your home and live there again, you might want to keep paying back capital.

How much can you borrow?

Before we get to how much, a quick refresh on two crucial concepts in the mortgage world (forgive us if you know this):

- **Loan-to-value (LTV).** Always shown as a percentage, this is the amount you borrow (the loan) as a proportion of the property's value. If you put down a 15% deposit, the loan-to-value will be 85%.
- **Equity.** This is how much you'd get if you sold your home and repaid the mortgage. It includes your deposit, capital you've repaid and any gains in price. If your 85% loan-to-value home, bought for £100,000, doubles in value, your equity will be £115,000 or 57.5%.

For most buy-to-let loans, lenders require both:

- **75% loan-to-value.** You need a deposit or equity of at least 25%. Though you might find the odd deal if you have only 15% or 20%, those rates will be extortionate
- **125%-145% rental cover.** Depending on the lender, the rent has to be at least 125%-145% more than your monthly mortgage payment calculated at a fictional higher interest rate, typically 5%-6%. Rules are tightening in the wake of the Brexit vote.

Buy-to-let mortgage calculator

How do you work out the maximum amount you can borrow? Here's a handy guide, based on the two requirements above:

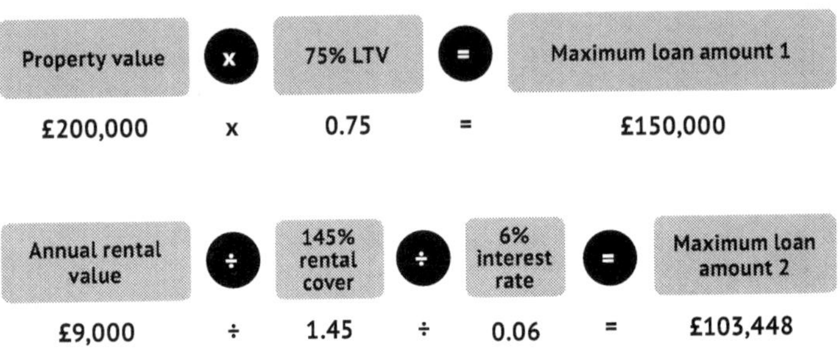

Buy-to-let mortgage providers will lend you the lower amount of these two calculations, as long as you, your property and your target tenants fit their criteria.

The plot thickens, though, for accidental landlords. If you have lived in your property or inherited it and now want to rent it out, under European Union rules lenders have to treat your mortgage as 'consumer buy-to-let' (as opposed to 'business buy-to-let' bought for investment purposes). Some will look at your earnings, and if you are older, you could struggle to get a loan. Generally, you may have less choice and end up paying a high rate. Of course, this may all change post Brexit.

Whether you are switching from a residential loan or applying for a buy-to-let mortgage on a new purchase, the process is the same. The bank will value both the property itself and its rental potential. If its surveyor thinks you want to borrow too much (or he was slapped with a parking ticket that morning), he could 'down-value' either of these – in which case you can appeal to the lender with comparable selling prices or agreed lets in the area. If the lender won't budge, you as an accidental landlord would have no choice but to put in more of your own money or sell up. And if you're buying? You can cough up the shortfall, try to get the seller to lower their price or walk away altogether.

What lenders require. Apart from the numbers, a lender will look at you, the property itself and the tenants you plan to put in it.

Balcony phobia scuppers loan

Call them bigots, but lenders don't like anything out of the ordinary – not even balconies. One client was refused a buy-to-let mortgage on his two-bedroom ex-council flat in a leafy part of southwest London because it had a balcony on the raised ground floor. It was 'a security risk'. (Never mind that if a door on the ground floor were such a big risk, three-quarters of homes in Britain would be unmortgageable.) Sadly, he ended up having to sell.

With a bog-standard buy-to-let purchase, lenders won't comb through every last soy latte receipt, as they'd have done for your residential mortgage. Nevertheless, they do have some basic criteria. *You* would be their dream client if you:

- Earn at least £25,000 as an employee (or £40,000 as joint applicants)
- Own your main home
- Have a spotless credit record
- Own a few rental properties, but not too many
- Are a UK resident.

In the light of that last point, what if you're an expat? It's tricky but not impossible: specialist brokers and private banks offer buy-to-let products that are not widely available. Thanks to all the extra hoop-jumping to prevent fraud, fees tend to be high and waiting times long. As ever, requirements vary. Some lend only to expats who live in specific countries or work for big multinationals; others want specific firms to certify your accounts.

Credit file error almost sinks deal

Good brokers make all the difference. Due to a bank blooper, our credit record once mistakenly showed that we had missed a mortgage payment on our main home. It came to light three years later as we were purchasing a buy-to-let flat – nearly causing the whole deal to collapse. Thanks to the intervention of our brilliant mortgage adviser, our bank fixed the error within a day and the purchase went ahead.

How to make yourself more creditworthy

- If you don't tick all the boxes, speak to a broker early to find out how you can boost your chances. The self-employed and business owners (like us) usually need around two years of accounts
- Before you approach any lender, check your credit report for any errors that could jeopardise your chances
- Don't apply for too many loans. Each application shows up on your credit report, and if there are too many, you'll get rejected by all.

Lenders also don't like non-standard homes. Their ideal *property*:

- Has a lease longer than 80 years (if it's leasehold)
- Is habitable with a working kitchen and bathroom
- Is not a flat above a shop or in a tower with more than five storeys
- Has a standard construction (not wood or concrete)
- Needs a loan of more than £40,000, so it's worth their bother.

As for *tenants*, in a now familiar refrain, lenders don't like non-standard ones. That means few will accept:

- Students, despite most of them having rent guarantors
- Renters on housing benefit, even though any tenant can start claiming this without telling you if they lose their job
- Unrelated sharers, though this depends on the number of rooms and whether they are on one contract or separate tenancies.

Lenders have been known to refuse mortgages when there are locks on bedroom doors, saying that the property could be let out by room – even when the landlord intends to let to a single family.

It gets even more complicated if criteria intersect. A self-employed accidental landlord wanting to let to students will have few options to choose from.

What to look for in a buy-to-let mortgage. Once you've narrowed it down to the lenders that will take you on, it's time to weigh up the options, considering:

- How much they'll lend you
- At what interest rate
- Whether said rate is fixed or variable. A rate that is fixed, typically for two to ten years, allows you to plan ahead with monthly payments that stay the same throughout. Of course, variable is better if you think rates will drop. This includes 'trackers' – pegged to Bank of England's rate – and 'standard variable rate' loans, which the lender can change whenever

they feel like it (though in practice they tend to follow the Bank rate)

- Fees, ahem. There are arrangement fees, valuation fees, legal fees (some force you to use a legal firm of their choice), exit fees, just-because-they-can fees...
- Nasty terms and restrictions in the fine print
- Penalties if you overpay or clear the loan early.

Yes, that's a lot of bullet points. Which drives home the point that there is more to choosing a buy-to-let mortgage than picking the lowest rate from a best-buy table. A good broker will be your new best friend.

Do you really need insurance?

Ah, insurance. It can be like a trophy wife: expensive, difficult to understand and what you get is not guaranteed. So, do you really need it? And if so, what kind?

We'll look at four main types of insurance that are relevant to you as a landlord:

- Buildings insurance
- Contents insurance (if your property is let furnished)
- Rent guarantee insurance
- Landlord liability insurance.

Buildings insurance

It's vital to have the right buildings insurance, which covers the structure of your property against fire, subsidence, floods and extreme weather. This is a condition of all mortgages, but even if you own outright, it's a risk not worth taking. Without cover, you stand to lose it all – and you'd still have to pay any mortgage.

Very important note: *your normal home insurance is likely to be invalid if you let out your property.* Check with your insurer that you have the right policy.

Good landlord buildings policies also cover loss of rent and temporary accommodation (for example, if a flood makes the house uninhabitable).

For a flat or leasehold property, the freeholder normally takes out buildings insurance. Ask them for a copy of the policy. Your lease will usually require you to tell your freeholder before you rent out your flat. Some also want the name and contact details of the tenants, as well as a copy of the tenancy agreement.

How much should I insure my building for?

Buildings insurance pays to repair or knock down and rebuild your property if it were to burn, subside or be damaged by extreme weather. The sum you're insured for is not the same as the property's market value; in fact, it's usually lower. It's your responsibility to double-check the sum is correct. If in doubt, ask a chartered surveyor – find one at ricsfirms.com. Over-insuring for more than the rebuild cost will not make a difference to any claim, but will push up your premiums.

The policy usually includes fixtures such as built-in wardrobes, kitchen surfaces, taps, basins, baths and showers. It also covers outbuildings, boundary walls, gates, pools, drives and paths. Clearly you'd only claim where the damage outweighs any excess on the policy and increased premiums on future policies.

Contents insurance

Landlord's contents insurance is particularly relevant if you let your property furnished, though it does also cover appliances and certain finishes such as carpets (yes, even fitted carpets) in unfurnished rentals. As policies usually have an excess and single item limit, it could make more sense to pay any repair costs yourself.

Your tenants are responsible for protecting their own belongings against loss or damage.

Rent guarantee insurance

In principle, this sounds like a great idea: the insurer pays your rent if your tenant doesn't. But watch the fine print – policies can kick in only after a month in arrears, then take a second month as excess, and proceed to tap the deposit first. Some limit the amount of rent that can be guaranteed (£2,500 a month, for example), the number of months (typically six) or the tenant type (no students, say). Many have to be renewed every time the tenancy is renewed, even with the same tenants.

If you do buy a rent guarantee policy, pick one that includes legal expenses to evict the tenant. There is no substitute for proper checks to choose reliable tenants in the first place, but even good tenants can lose a job, fall ill or split up with a partner and stop paying rent. This insurance can give useful peace of mind (at a price).

Landlord liability insurance

What if a tenant or tradesman falls down the stairs, breaks a leg and sues you? Though the risk might be small, sums could be large – which is where landlord liability insurance comes in. This can often be added on to your buildings policy at little extra charge.

Should you use an insurance broker?

Insurance seems like an easy thing to buy online where you'll get the lowest prices. If you miss something among the myriad terms and conditions, however, it's just as easy to end up with an inappropriate or even invalid policy.

Our advice is to speak to a trusted broker. Though they may cost more, they can lead you through the maze of fine print to find the right policy. Plus – and this is a big plus – they can help you wade through the treacle of subsequent claims.

Insurance claims

Almost all policies require you to inform the insurer immediately (or 'put them on notice') in the event of a potential claim. Doing this too late could give your insurer grounds to refuse or reduce your claim. Don't leave that gap: tell them quickly and do it in writing. If you're not certain there will be a claim, contact your insurer or broker anyway just to check.

Submitting a claim can sap your will to live with endless forms and hapless call-centre staff, only to hear 'Computer says no' many months later. This is where having bought via a broker can prove extremely useful: they can help you submit a claim.

If you feel you have a valid claim that insurers have rejected, contact the Financial Ombudsman Service for advice on how to complain (financial-ombudsman.org.uk).

Phew. With the right mortgage and insurance cover in the bag, your property is now all the safer. Now for – drum roll – tax. And then we're done with money matters. Promise.

CHAPTER 4

Think ahead to save a fortune in tax

In this chapter:

- **What you can and can't deduct from your rental income**
- **Should you set up a company? Plus, easier ways to be tax efficient**
- **How to save thousands of pounds in capital gains tax when you sell**
- **The tax lowdown for landlords who live abroad.**

The taxman used to be rather kind to property owners. Then came the Great Buy-to-let Bashing of 2015, in which the Chancellor announced several tax changes to give first-time buyers a leg up against investors. Cue predictions that as many as 500,000 buy-to-lets would be sold off – you'd have thought that the end was nigh for rentals.

So how bad is it? Yes, it's getting harder to make a profit after tax. And yes, if you're a higher-rate taxpayer with a big mortgage, it could get impossible. Yet Armageddon it is not.

Before you panic and put your property up for sale, you need to do the maths (or get an expert to help) to see how the changes will affect your bottom line. In this section we will walk you through the basic principles, so you can start thinking how they apply to your situation. This will help you decide whether to sell or hold – and if you hold, how to do it tax efficiently.

However, *this is not a tax book*. Don't base your plans on what you read here – this is only a first step. Tax rules change often. Though they tend to be simple in themselves, the mind can start to boggle when they intersect. When Daniel was a bachelor and employee with one rental flat, it took him an hour to add his property income to his tax return. Now that we're married with a business, several properties, dividends and other income, a good tax specialist does it for us – saving us thousands of pounds. Tax is one area where expert advice is worth every penny. Don't leave (or sell) your home without it.

Your tax obligations

First things first. When you start letting out a property, you have to tell HMRC that you have a new income source from which they can squeeze money. Though they have no automatic way of finding out about this, don't be tempted to keep schtum. As part of a clamp-down on lettings tax evasion, HMRC gets data from estate agents, deposit protection schemes and local authorities.

How do you tell them? You need to register for self-assessment tax returns (even if you normally get taxed through your employer) and file a return every year. On the property pages, fill in your rental income, deduct allowable costs (listed below) and add the profit to the rest of your income to see how much tax you should pay. This is all pretty straightforward, but if you're short on time or confidence, by all means get an accountant to do it for you.

HMRC's own advisers can also give more detail on what is allowed. Contact them via hmrc.gov.uk or their telephone helpline.

Ignore the taxman at your peril

Accidental landlords Ketan and Priya are among more than 10,000 landlords who owned up about undisclosed rental income as part of an HMRC campaign. The couple started letting out their Sheffield home after Ketan's job at the head office of an insurance company moved from the Steel City to Birmingham, but they failed to tell the taxman. Three years on, the tax due on their 'it's just temporary' rental was £3,000. Because they came clean voluntarily, they only got a 20% fine on top of that. Had they been caught out, it would have been a 100% penalty and possible prosecution.

What can you deduct?

They say no one is ever as modest about their income as when they're filling in their tax return. Jokes aside, when it comes to tax the name of the game is to deduct every cost you legitimately can. If you're a 40% higher-rate taxpayer, every £100 expense you claim could cut your tax bill by £40.

So what can you claim?

Capital expenses. The buying costs (the property itself, stamp duty, legal fees, surveys) plus any work to improve the property, such as an extension. Inflation takes all the fun out of these: you can deduct them only once you sell the property, by which time the solicitor's bill you filed 20 years ago might stretch to a packet of Maltesers.

Revenue expenses. Now you're talking. As long as they are for letting your property, you can deduct all running costs from your rental profit as you go along.

What are legitimate revenue expenses? You can claim just about every cost after the point of buying your property, for example:

- Repairs that *restore the property to its previous condition* rather than making it better. This includes painting, double glazing (you're usually not allowed to fit single glazing nowadays) or even updating a bathroom or kitchen to a more modern look without making it bigger. Works done up to seven years before the property is let out also qualify, if you can show they are for the purpose of preparing the property to let. An accidental landlord could claim for repainting their home just before they move out, but not for that shiny new kitchen island fitted six years prior
- Letting agent fees and advertising
- Furniture bought for the property
- Service charges and ground rents
- Insurance
- Deposit protection fees, gas safety checks and energy performance certificates
- Utility, cleaning or gardening bills paid by you
- Accountancy fees
- Legal advice, for example on your tenancy agreement
- Bad debts.

Some less obvious, more general expenses also qualify:

- Relevant costs up to *seven years before* you start letting out your first property, such as tax advice
- Professional fees, such as for a landlord association
- Travel, phone calls, postage and food (but not your time) while running your property business
- A portion of household bills if you run said business from home
- Education (yes, even this book).

There is pressure on the government to reduce the allowable expenses, so it's best to check with your accountant for any changes.

Of course you don't want to incur costs just to save tax, but you do want to keep good records so you can make costs count. You have to hold on to all receipts for six years. To ease bookkeeping, open a separate current account solely for your property. And if you hire one firm to do both improvements and repairs (a loft conversion and a repaint, say), ask them to separate out the invoices.

Are you still awake? Have you spotted the missing item on our long list of allowable expenses above? (Hint: it's probably your biggest cost.) Which brings us to...

The mortgage interest mess

Thanks to the Great Buy-to-let Bashing of 2015, mortgage interest payments – a legitimate cost of doing business – are no longer on that list. (The then Chancellor also slapped an extra 3% on stamp duty on all buy-to-let purchases. These two changes would explain a reported spike in landlords buying dartboards sporting George Osborne's face.) A landlord campaign aided by Cherie Blair, the former prime minister's wife whose family company owns at least 27 buy-to-let flats, is lobbying the government about the mortgage interest tax changes (tenanttax.co.uk). If they succeed, you can skip this bit with a sigh of relief.

But for now, back to the facts. From April 2020, you can *no longer deduct mortgage interest as an expense before you work out your profit*. Instead, you apply a *20% relief after* you've arrived at your profit but before you calculate your tax.

It took us (and most pundits) a few days to get our heads around it. In a nutshell, it means:

- Most 20% basic-rate taxpayers end up the same
- Everyone else pays more. Worse, 40% higher-rate payers with big mortgages can end up paying more in tax than they actually make. Yes, really
- Taxable profits are higher for all, because you can't deduct interest before you arrive at them. This could push 20% basic-rate payers on to the borderline of the 40% higher-rate band – even if they are barely profitable.

An example makes this clearer:

Taxable profit

£11,000 rental income

[£7,500 mortgage interest *not deducted*]

- £1,000 other costs

= £10,000 taxable profit

Allowance: 20% of £7,500 interest = £1,500 relief

Basic-rate tax

20% tax on £10,000 profit = £2,000

Allowance applied: £2,000 - £1,500 relief = £500 tax

You have left in your pocket: £10,000 profit - £7,500 interest - £500 tax = £2,000

Higher-rate tax

40% tax on £10,000 profit = £4,000

Allowance applied: £4,000 - £1,500 relief = £2,500 tax

You have left in your pocket: £10,000 profit - £7,500 interest - 2,500 tax = £0

If the interest were any higher, this higher-rate taxpayer would pay more in tax than she would have left over.

As of 2016, your interest payments are still deductible in full. However, the new method will be phased in gradually over four years from April 2017. Good luck on working out your tax in the meantime – it's not for the faint of heart (or head).

Should you set up a company?

There is one loophole in the new tax rule on mortgage interest: it only applies to individuals. Companies can still deduct interest from profits as before – for now. No wonder the number of buy-to-let mortgages issued to companies doubled after the change was announced. So, should you join the rush and move your existing rental property to a company?

To do this, you'd have to 'sell' your property to your new company at market rate. This means you would have to not only pay capital gains tax on any increase in the property's value, but your company would then have to cough up the 3% higher stamp duty rate on second homes. Ouch.

Is it worth buying new properties through a company? Not if you're a basic-rate taxpayer, except perhaps in borderline cases. Even for higher-rate payers it would likely only make sense if you're planning to leave returns to build up in the company, such as for a pension pot or to fund your next property. Otherwise it could end up costing you more.

But, as with most things tax, there is no blanket answer. Here's what to consider:

- As a company, you'll pay corporation tax rather than income tax on your profit – so higher-rate taxpayers will more than halve their tax bill from 2017
- If you extract your rental profits, you have to do so as dividends. If these are more than £5,000, you'll be taxed a second time on this, which could leave you worse off
- Companies have no capital gains tax allowance, so you pay more when you sell
- Borrowing costs for companies are around 0.7% higher
- There are extra costs and hassle to file annual company accounts.

The right answer for you depends on what you earn, how much you're borrowing, how you want to use the rental profit, if you want to sell and a myriad other factors. Do take expert advice.

Five ways to save income tax

There are simpler ways than setting up a company to be tax efficient:

1. If you are married, make sure the lower earner owns the rental property – or most of it – to benefit from a lower tax band. You can transfer property between spouses through a simple legal process, without paying any tax. Profit is split proportionally to your ownership, as long as you inform HMRC through a special form that the split is not 50/50.
2. Even if you have the funds to pay off your buy-to-let mortgage, it usually makes sense not to do so: you can then still claim the relief on mortgage interest payments, where you'd otherwise pay more in tax.
3. To help your cash flow, time big revenue expenses to be in a tax year when you would have made a profit.
4. Carry forward any remaining losses until they are 'wiped out' by profits. With a bit of planning, this can save you thousands of pounds over several years.
5. Lucky enough to own multiple rental homes? Offset losses on one against profits on the rest, as your tax liability is calculated across your whole property portfolio. However, you can't offset against other income sources.

Tax due when you sell

Capital gains tax (CGT) is only due when you sell your rental property. You pay this on the difference between the prices you bought and sold for, minus any expenses:

Buying costs. Remember that solicitor's bill you've kept for 20 years? Now you can deduct all your capital expenses: the property purchase price, stamp duty, legal fees, surveys and any improvement work, such as a loft conversion.

Selling costs. Likewise, you can deduct the estate agent's commission, advertising costs and legal fees for the property's sale.

Before you work out CGT, you can also deduct your allowances. For accidental landlords, this includes two generous reliefs because you've lived in your home:

- **Annual allowance.** Every year, everyone gets their first £11,100 (for 2015/16 and 2016/17) in gains tax-free. To make the most of this, time your sale to be in a tax year when you don't have other capital gains.
- **Principal private residence relief.** You pay no CGT on all the time you've lived in the property, plus the last one and a half years. You can extend this for periods when it was uninhabitable because of works, or if your job took you elsewhere. Also, the relief can apply to two properties for overlapping periods, as long as you can prove that you genuinely lived in both and told HMRC which was your main one within two years.
- **Private letting relief.** If you let out your former main home, you get up to £40,000 in gains tax free.

Double your relief if you're married

Married joint owners can claim *all three CGT allowances for both spouses*. Before you sell, use a simple legal process to transfer ownership between the two of you to maximise your relief. As spouses you won't pay any tax on such a transfer, but it could save you tens of thousands of pounds in CGT.

Tax if you live overseas

If you live abroad for six months or more while renting out a UK home, HMRC classes you as a 'non-resident landlord'. You have to pay income tax in one of two ways. You either receive your rent in full and pay tax through self-assessment – to do this, you have to apply for approval from HMRC (gov.uk/tax-uk-income-live-abroad/rent) – or your lettings agent or tenant has to deduct your tax and pay it to HMRC. This is a hassle for all of you, as you could easily pay too much or too little tax.

If you sell your property while living abroad, you also have to pay capital gains tax on any gains after 5 April 2015. You have to tell HMRC about the sale within 30 days of its completion, even if you've made a loss.

Tax if you rent out a room

If you let out a furnished room, or even a whole floor (but not a separate flat), in your home to a lodger, you can earn up to £7,500 a year tax free under the **Rent-a-room Scheme**. 'Woohoo,' you may say. Yes, but there are a few things to watch out for to keep woohoo from turning into whoops:

- If you claim this allowance, *you can't deduct any expenses*. You have to include all extra charges such as cleaning, bills, meals and laundry to give the total figure for rental income from your lodger. So if you have a lot of expenses, you may be better off not claiming the Rent-a-room allowance but treating the whole lot as ordinary rental income instead, from which you then deduct expenses to arrive at a taxable profit. Every year you can use whichever option works better for you
- You don't have to fill in a tax return if you earn less than £7,500 from your lodger – the allowance will then automatically apply. However, you must file a return for earnings over £7,500

- If you share the rental income with someone else, you each get half of the £7,500 allowance.

When you have a lodger, you are still responsible for the full **council tax**. You must tell your council if having them in the house means you're no longer entitled to a single person discount.

If you have more than one lodger at a time, you may have to pay **capital gains tax** when you sell on the part of the house that you rented out, for the time it was let. That's because the taxman sees that as running a lodging business, so you'll lose some of the tax relief that applies to price gains on your main home.

Well done for resisting the temptation to iron your socks rather than read this far. Now that you understand the basic property tax rules, you can start planning ahead. Whatever your situation, get expert tax advice both before you start letting out your home and ahead of selling it. It could save you many thousands of pounds. In fact, this chapter will likely save you more money than any other.

With that sorted, we can talk about more interesting things (read: almost anything else).

CHAPTER 5

Do you need an agent?

PLAN

In this chapter

- **What to weigh up in your decision to use a lettings agent or do it yourself**
- **Ten ways to self-manage effectively with clever tools and systems**
- **The lowdown on the new generation of online agents**
- **Good, bad or ugly? Twenty questions to help you pick the best high-street agent.**

To manage or not to manage, that is the question. Do you let and manage your rental property yourself – there are plenty of new online services that can help – or use an agent? And how on earth do you find a good one?

There are lots of scary stories of agents who take your money but do a terrible job of looking after your property. You may well know someone who has experienced this first-hand.

Agent fails to spot dead seller

One agent showed prospective buyers around a Notting Hill house without realising that the 55-year-old owner, whom he thought was asleep on the sofa, had actually died. The agent admitted to a coroner's court that 'something didn't seem right' but he continued with the viewing nevertheless, reports the *Daily Mail*.

Why does the industry get such bad press? Having built Swift into a trusted lettings agency, Daniel has seen the pitfalls first hand:

- Britain offers degrees in Viking Studies and Knitting Design, but you need no qualifications to be an agent or run an agency
- Unlike sales, profit margins in lettings are low once you've paid for the fancy shopfront and branded cars. Most agencies cannot afford to pay well so staff can be inexperienced and staff turnover is high
- Many charge their fees upfront as a lump sum, so have no incentive to look after a property proactively once they've got their money.

Because of all this, lettings agents may focus on short-term profit instead of long-term service. Most of the time a landlord will be none the wiser if the agent just sticks the first available tenant into the property rather than finding the best fit. Nor will they know how slow the agent is to respond to a tenant's maintenance query.

That's why many landlords prefer to let and manage (or just manage) their own properties rather than hand them over to an agent. But it's not always possible to do it yourself (for instance, if you live far away) and a good agent can make a big difference to your peace of mind and profits.

Even if you use an agent for everything, you can't be completely hands-off. This is a business, after all, and to get the most out of it you need to know how it works. Plus, you are still liable for your agent's mistakes: a forgotten gas safety check or deposit registration is an 'oops, sorry' for them and a huge headache for you.

Far more important than whether to self-manage or use an agent is to *self-manage effectively* or use the *right agent*.

What to weigh up

If you're not sure whom to put in charge of your property, here are the factors to consider:

Time. How much time do you have? And how do you value your time? It takes Swift around eight hours of work to find tenants, another two to four hours per month to manage a property, plus five or so to end a tenancy – and that's with all the systems in place. Over a year-long rental at £1,000 a month, a 10% fee equates to £25 an hour – and if any problems arise, it becomes even cheaper. Unless you earn less than that, live nearby and have the time and energy to deal with boilers, bedbugs and break clauses, a good agent is a bargain.

Own a 'low-maintenance' new build? Even with no repairs, there will still be admin and contractual issues. No matter how trouble-free you think your property might be, managing it well always takes time and focus.

Too busy for the bother

Despite living near their rental flat in central London, Fran and Victor opted to have it fully managed by an agent. With two young children and busy work schedules, they factored the extra cost into the rental return to save time and stay at arms' length from their tenants.

Cost. Usually the main reason why landlords self-manage. You will save a fair bit in agent fees, but remember that these fees are tax deductible from your rental income so the saving might be less than you think.

Let-only deal saves a packet on posh rental

Although they were living abroad, John and Lily chose not to use a managing agent for their upmarket west London family home. Instead, they asked their parents who lived nearby to ensure any maintenance was done to the right standard. As the rent was high, this saved them a lot in management commission. They also negotiated a good lettings-only deal with their local agent.

Arms' length or up close? Doing viewings yourself could help you find a better tenant: unspoken clues when meeting them in person tell you much more than a paper reference. You can also build rapport, which will help you get the best out of tenant.

On the other hand, a skilled agent could get a higher rent and defuse any disputes because they're at arms' length. You also might want to keep your details private. Plus, you won't field the call about the broken boiler or leaking roof on Christmas Eve (as we have), nor will you have to deal with tenants who bother you with non-emergencies at 11pm (like the one who locked herself out, called in a panic to beg for keys, then got in – but failed to update the agent who had travelled an hour to her aid).

Control. No one knows your property as well as you do. Looking after it yourself lets you see maintenance issues first-hand, so you can make the right choices and use your own preferred tradesmen.

Enjoyment. Are you forever fixing things? Do you love leaping into action to solve a tenant crisis? If that's you, you might enjoy self-managing even if it makes little sense financially. Equally, if you're the hands-off type who hires a handyman to oil a squeaky door, it won't be for you.

Precision (and patience). It's not particularly complicated to let and manage your property yourself. However, there are lots and lots of annoying little boxes to tick. (Hey, we've filled a book with them.) The consequences of getting it wrong can be serious. If attention to detail is not one of your strengths, you might be better off getting an agent who knows their stuff to do it for you.

Your situation could of course change – perhaps you'll grow to have less time and more money. The right decision now might not be the right decision in five years. Whatever you decide, don't underestimate how much time and effort it takes to manage well.

Ten ways to self-manage effectively

Self-management needn't be an all-or-nothing choice. Rather, think of it as a sliding scale – you can outsource as much or as little as you like while still retaining control. Here are some ideas:

1. **Tenant finding.** In the past tenants used to find homes mainly by visiting a local estate agency; now most start their search online via portals such as Rightmove, Zoopla and OnTheMarket. As a landlord you can now advertise your property on these portals through online agents such as OpenRent.co.uk, Upad.co.uk or easyProperty.com from as little as £10 a week. Most will expect you to host your own viewings, though some charge around £80 an hour to do it for you. You can then bolt on a pick-and-mix of admin and paperwork.
2. **Advert content.** A professional property photographer charges £50–£125 for a set of photos. Some photographers do floorplans, too, for £20–£30, or ask the assessor who does your energy performance certificate to help with this. Once you've written your advert wording, keep this on file along with the photos and floorplan to reuse.
3. **Referencing.** Even if you farm out nothing else, get a company to do this for you. Online specialists charge £20–£30 to do all the checks that would take you hours; search 'tenant referencing' to find one.
4. **Inventory.** Without an inventory by an independent clerk, you'll have a hard time making any deposit deductions. It costs around £100 (for a two-bedroom one-bathroom furnished flat) to create at the start of your first tenancy, then another £80 (for the same size flat) at each new check-in. Find a clerk through the Association of Professional Inventory Providers (apip.org.uk). If you still want to do this laborious task yourself, use an app for it – that speeds up the process considerably.
5. **Repairs.** If DIY is not your forte, you'll need a good handyman on speed dial. To avoid waiting in to meet him every time, fit a key safe outside your rental property. You could also give him a set of keys; some maintenance firms offer a free key-holding service.

Setting up systems, too, will free you up from doing dreary tasks to focus on what matters to you:

6. **Go paperless.** Scan and store all your documents in electronic folders on a searchable platform such as Google Drive or Evernote. No more thumbing through piles of paperwork ever again. Include notes on where the stop cock, fuse box and meters are; how the heating and appliances work; bins and parking spaces; and which types of paint, tiles and carpet you used in each room. You can also store marketing and maintenance photos here.
7. **Sign contracts online.** Save hours by signing tenancy agreements through secure digital services such as HelloSign (free), DocuSign or Adobe Sign (both subscription-based).
8. **Diarise dates.** At the start of a new tenancy, put key dates in your electronic calendar: gas safety checks, inspections, when to send out end of tenancy notices and when to negotiate a renewal. This two-minute task can save you a lot of trouble down the line.
9. **Rent collection alerts.** Get your tenants to set up a standing order for the rent to land in your account on the first day of the month – that makes it easier to check for late payments. Or be in control by setting up a direct debit via gocardless.com: it costs £2 per payment and notifies you if it is cancelled.
10. **Record conversations.** Note down what you've discussed with tenants, tradesmen, agents and freeholders. Google Keep or Evernote works well for this.

Using an online agent

As we've seen above, you can use the new generation of online agents to advertise your property. They can, however, take care of a whole lot more: some offer full management at a mere 3% of your rent. Tempted?

Though there are well-funded players (easyProperty.com and Purplebricks.com) and brands with excellent reviews (OpenRent.co.uk and Upad.co.uk), there are also wannabes trying to jump on the band-wagon. As with any business, vet your online agent carefully. If the fees sound too good to be true, they probably are.

On the upside, they do bring competition to a market that has a lot of fat in it. We doubt that traditional high-street agents will be totally replaced, but they are certainly being forced to raise their game. In sales especially, online agents can offer incredible savings: traditional agents charge their sales fee as a percentage of the property value, but is it really 10 times more work to sell a two-bedroom flat in Chelsea, London, than the same size property in Bradford? Surely not. Lettings, however, require an ongoing relationship.

You may not be confident enough to use an online agent the first time you rent out your property, but they do open up more options for you as a landlord. Some of their advantages are:

- **Lower costs,** usually the top reason for going digital
- **Pick and mix services.** You can buy only the services you need
- **Transparency.** It's usually easier to track the progress of your rental as you can do so online at any time
- **Control.** You remain in charge of the process, rather than having to rely on agents to drive things forward.

If you want to use an online agent, what do you look out for?

- Check what exactly is included. Hosted viewings, for one, usually aren't. When you add all the costs together, it could actually work out more expensive
- Local 'experts' can cover very wide geographic areas. In reality, most are not area experts at all
- You can't go into a local agent's office to demand better service when you feel you've been let down, so it's more difficult to hold an online agent to account
- The flip side of being in control is that using an online agent can be a lot more stressful if it all relies on you

- Dealing with maintenance issues can be complex. It's unlikely someone in a call-centre who's never been to your property will do an optimal job of deciding what to do.

The exclusively online agent didn't exist a number of years ago, but is now a rapidly growing sector likely to 'disrupt the market', as their business leaders like to put it. In the long run, landlords should be the better for it.

Using a high-street agent

Lettings agents don't have the best of names. (You have two bullets. Who do you shoot: the lawyer, the insurance salesman or the estate agent? The estate agent – twice, just to make sure.) Yet there are some excellent high-street agencies that could prove invaluable. Their biggest benefit is that – for a fee – they take care of all the details for you, so you don't need to worry about a thing.

How, then, do you tell the professional experts from the suits who sold wet fish last week? We've put together 20 points to sift your shortlist, based on Daniel's insider view of how the industry really works:

1. **A personal thumbs-up trumps all.** If you know a landlord who trusts their agent after years of service, you're on to a winner. Failing that, ask to speak to a few clients of the agent you are considering. A good one won't refuse to give referees.
2. **Check independent reviews.** Ratings on Google are hard to fake. All Agents (allagents.co.uk) allows people to rate their estate agents, but does not verify users so is open to tenants leaving malicious reviews.
3. **Steer clear of flash chains.** There's nothing wrong with branches, but you're the one who'll pay for those funky coffee machines and fridges full of sparkling water. Also, staff turnover tends to be high, especially in lettings – often seen as the poor cousin of the more glamorous sales business. Certainly give the brush off to anyone claiming to have 20 merchant bankers with glowing

references queuing up to rent your property. If possible, opt for a specialist lettings agency.

How many agents does it take to flush a loo?

We appreciate that Rome wasn't built in a day, but according to Wikipedia, in six weeks they were able to construct a fully functional aqueduct. This is exactly the same period in which [agency] *has been unable to fix a small porcelain toilet. Whilst I'm not comparing the size of the Roman Empire to the Battersea branch of* [agency], *you guys do have notable advantages such as electricity, phone lines and an oversized fridge stuffed with Perrier.*

Extracted from a tenant's email to their lettings agent, part of an (in)famous chain.

Fees

4. **Clear fees.** Since 2014, it is a legal requirement for estate agents to list their fees on their website and marketing material. If they don't comply (and 14% don't, according to the campaign group Generation Rent), it doesn't bode well for them helping you to comply with the 140-plus lettings laws.
5. **No hidden extras.** Ask the agent to explain their full rate card. Do they charge extra for inventories, contracts or deposit protection? (See info panel below for full list.) Your tenants won't be happy if they're slapped with high tenancy renewal charges.
6. **Upfront or monthly?** If an agent takes their fees for management only after the monthly rent comes in, instead of a lump sum upfront, they are incentivised to be proactive. For a let-only service, the agent will normally want their full commission upfront, which can exceed a month's rent and leave you out of pocket. Check what happens if the tenant then leaves early: is any portion of this commission refundable?

7. **Check the fine print.** Will you still need to pay commission when the property is vacant?

The going rates

Average rates on the high street range from 5–10% (plus Vat) for let-only to 10–17% (plus Vat) for a full lettings and property management service. Agents also make money by charging for extras, some of which may be passed on to the tenant:

- **Inventory, check-in and check-out:** £75–£200 at both check-in and check-out
- **Contract fee:** £0–£450
- **Deposit protection.** Some agents will pass on the small charge for the deposit insurer's policy
- **Tenancy renewal.** As much as 15% for little more than printing a contract. Avoid this by asking for the tenancy to roll on into a periodic one
- **Maintenance float.** Some require a money float to cover repairs.

Fees charged to tenants vary widely, from nothing to £780 for two people by one agent in central London, found a survey by Generation Rent.

Marketing

8. **On which portals?** Agents should advertise on two out of the three big property portals (Rightmove, Zoopla and OnTheMarket). A silly turf war currently being waged means no agent can be on all three.
9. **Professional adverts.** What do their property listings look like? A cat in the bath, a lone prosthetic leg on the dining

table or living room that looks like a tip – all real-life examples snapped by lazy agents on their phones – should not be among the photos. Adverts need to include floorplans but no typos or gobbledygook in the wording.

Maintenance

10. **Who does repairs?** Large agencies usually have a central team that runs your property maintenance, although they won't necessarily let you know this. This can be efficient for them, but not for you: someone unfamiliar with your property can make costly decisions that are not in your best interests. Check how they screen repair requests to make sure the boiler really is broken, not just off, before sending a tradesman. Who do they call: their own people, trusted suppliers or just someone off the web? Do they check appropriate professional membership and insurance? Smaller agencies usually work with a few local tradesmen who get to know your property on repeat visits and can be held accountable if there are problems.
11. **No kick-backs.** Ask directly whether the agency gets commission from its maintenance suppliers. This practice is fairly widespread – in fact, more than 50 landlords lodged a £2.2 million court case against Foxtons over kick-backs after the agency charged £616 – including a £203 mark-up – to fit a security light for a London landlord. A good agent should not be doing this, or should at least be prepared to disclose it.
12. **Regular inspections.** How frequently does the agent visit your property to inspect it?
13. **Emergency procedure.** Do they have a phone number for after-hours emergencies? How quickly will they be on the scene if, say, a water pipe bursts?
14. **Repair costs.** Do they clear the cost of repairs with you first? Is there any amount below which they just go ahead?

Transparency

15. **Terms of business.** You'd be amazed at how many agencies don't have a contract with their terms of business. This sounds warnings bells.

16. **Financial safeguards.** Does the agent have a separate client bank account for all client monies? Do they have client money protection in place so they can't run off with the rent? (This will become a legal requirement soon.) How often do they send out statements?

Legal requirements

17. **Gas safety check.** Does the agent organise the annual test by a gas engineer? You are responsible for this, so make sure they do.

18. **Deposit protection.** Likewise, how do they prove that they have protected your tenants' deposits? You are liable if they forget.

Professional bodies

19. **Redress scheme.** Since 2014, all lettings agents have to belong to one of three government-approved redress schemes (The Property Ombudsman, the Property Redress Scheme or Ombudsman Services Property). If they can't abide by their own rules...

20. **Trade bodies.** Membership of the multitude of other professional organisations is voluntary. (See info panel below for full list.) Confusingly, these bodies perform different and sometimes overlapping functions. Each has its own code of conduct to which you'd have recourse if your agent is a member, but spot-checks can be rare. ARLA and RICS require certain qualifications; others simply entail paying a membership each year. Don't award too many points for this.

Professional bodies for lettings agents

- Association of Residential Letting Agents (arla.co.uk)
- National Association of Estate Agents (naea.co.uk)
- National Landlords Association (landlords.org.uk)
- The Property Ombudsman (tpos.co.uk)
- Residential Landlords Association (rla.org.uk)
- Royal Institution of Chartered Surveyors (rics.org)
- SAFEagent (safeagents.co.uk)
- UK Association of Letting Agents (ukala.org.uk).

By grilling agents on these 20 points, you'll hopefully avoid ending up with one who thinks 'asap' means four weeks Thursday or treats a holding deposit as their quarterly bonus. However, even top-notch agencies can slip up and the buck stops with you.

With all this in mind, you can now make an informed decision on whether to use a traditional agent, try an online one or do it yourself. You can also factor these extra costs or extra time into your plan.

Whichever route you take, you still need to know how lettings and maintenance work so that you can make good decisions and steer the process throughout. That brings us to our next P: property – all you need to know on preparing your home for letting.

Part 2
Property

CHAPTER 6

Prep and promote your property

In this chapter:

- **When to let furnished, and when not to, with insider advice on what to provide**
- **Ten simple ways to increase your property's appeal**
- **How to make your advert stand out from the online crowd**
- **What to do if your home is still not letting.**

Daniel's rule number one of lettings: *properties attract the tenants they deserve.* Put the odds in your favour by doing all you can to make your property look its best.

Before we get to the dos and don'ts of marketing, we'll go over how you can prepare your place. (Spoiler alert: no chipped crockery, yoga mats or toupees in biscuit tins, please!)

Furnished or unfurnished?

In most countries rental properties are provided without any furniture – and if you do want it furnished, you'll pay a premium. In fact, in Germany tenants have to bring their own kitchen – cabinets, appliances and all – as most rentals have an empty shell for a kitchen.

It's a fairly unique quirk of Britain that fully furnished properties usually let for the same as unfurnished ones (unless they are top-end). Storage space is in short supply and it's a pain to squeeze large pieces of furniture through narrow doors and tight staircases. As a result, most landlords simply prefer to leave furniture in situ. Getting rid of it is a grudge expense. Nor do landlords like spending money on buying furniture, as that's a sunk cost.

However, your decision to furnish should not be driven by your preference, but by your property type and its tenant profile. Successful landlords work *with* demand rather than fighting it. For example, students in university towns such as Cambridge or Southampton will expect flats to be fully furnished, while families in wealthy suburbs usually have their own furniture so prefer to rent empty houses. The older and more financially established the tenant, the more likely they are to want an unfurnished property to fill with their own belongings.

My dog chewed my home's work

When twenty-something Jacob first put his two-bedroom bachelor pad in, southwest London up for rent, he didn't bother fixing the skirting board and vinyl kitchen floor that his terrier had chewed so enthusiastically. He also removed his surround sound system, but left the wires dangling from the walls. The bathroom floor had started to wobble because of a leak from the shower, but he thought nothing of it – until his flat sat empty for a month. After a lecture from his lettings agent, Jacob fixed all the snags and, hey presto, the flat was snapped up by two young professional women who wouldn't have given it a second look in its old state.

Ask your local estate agent what the typical tenant for your property prefers. But be flexible: there are always exceptions. Being willing to buy a sofa or get rid of a bed at a tenant's request can often make the difference between agreeing a let or not.

If there is no clear market preference, our strong advice is to supply a property unfurnished. This leaves less to break or replace, and tenants who've brought in their own furniture may well end up staying longer.

Can you store your own stuff somewhere in the property?

In principle, yes. It's your house and you can negotiate any storage clauses in the contract. But we wouldn't recommend it. Tenants can resent being excluded from part of 'their' home – not a good start to a tenancy. Also, it's inevitably that locked loft or garage that becomes the source of a leak, pest or faulty wiring. If your lettings agent holds the key, this can delay emergency access. Yet if the key is hidden at the property, the tenant can find out (and some have been known to 'break in'). Don't assume total security.

What exactly should (and shouldn't) you provide?

Even **unfurnished** lets are not completely empty. You still need to provide:

- **Appliances.** Just about 99% of tenants will expect a decent washing machine, fridge-freezer and cooker
- **Light fittings** for wall and ceiling lights
- **Curtains or blinds.** Tenants will need these from day one, but finding the right size is a hassle, so do supply them. Go with neutral or understated colours and use poles rather than tracks for curtains as the latter tend to break
- **Household basics.** As a courtesy provide doormats to protect your floors, new loo brushes, dustbins, a few cleaning materials and loo rolls.

For **furnished** rentals, remove anything financially or sentimentally valuable to you. Also take out that glass table or white sofa that could easily get damaged.

But leave behind any specific items that you sourced to fit into quirky spaces. This can make the place feel bigger or help define zones in an open-plan kitchen/living room. Furnished lets should include everything listed above for unfurnished ones, plus:

Large furniture	Tenants will expect beds, mattresses, wardrobes and a chest of drawers in each bedroom. In the living room, supply sofas (with washable loose covers) and possibly a dining table and chairs.
Garden furniture	A table and chairs is a nice addition to any garden. Consider a retractable washing line to encourage drying laundry outside – and cut condensation indoors.
Artwork	Apart from maybe a mirror that fits above an imposing mantelpiece, tenants will prefer to hang their own choice of art. But at the lower end of the market they may not have the funds, so may want a few pictures. Consult them, but certainly don't leave any valuable artwork.
Lamps, side tables and accessories	These come down to personal taste – yes, even the candles and vases that you think will add ambiance. They won't bag you any more rent, so better to remove them.
TV	With the exception of built-in TVs, let tenants provide their own. TVs are relatively inexpensive nowadays, but if they break it's a hassle for you to fix or replace them.

Vacuum cleaner	Don't. Again, it won't get you any more rent and the tenants will expect you to repair or replace it if it stops working.
Small electrical appliances	Another no. Besides the repair issue, toasters, kettles and irons pose a fire or electrical risk. Any such items should be tested regularly, creating more cost and hassle.
Crockery and bed linen	No. This is only an expectation if it's a short let or a serviced apartment at the very top end.

When furnishing a property, less is more: a few good pieces are better than a house full of wobbly leftovers. Tenants will style to their taste with their own accessories, so you only need to supply the large key items. *Whatever you do provide has to be kept maintained and safe.*

If you need to furnish a property quickly from scratch, you could consider using one of the many landlord furniture pack suppliers. (Search 'landlord furniture'.) They can deliver a coordinated set to fill a two-bedroom flat from around £1,500 the very next day. These firms hold large amounts of stock and negotiate discounts because they buy in bulk, so you could end up paying less than if you sourced it all yourself – without having to wait in, miss deliveries and fight with missing bits of flat-pack.

Prefer to do it yourself? Invest in an electric screwdriver to speed up assembly. Although Ikea is simultaneously our nation's favourite and most despised store, it's a great source of furniture for rental properties (see info panel below). The nature of flat-pack also means that it can easily be brought into properties with narrow doorways or winding corridors.

PROPERTY

Little black book of lettings supplies

Appliances. Ao.com delivers next day and removes old appliances at the same time. John Lewis (johnlewis.com) offers longer guarantees but often won't collect the old appliances on the same visit – which means more hassle and longer lead times.

New furniture. Ikea's better ranges, such as Besta shelving, Ektorp and Stocksund sofas, are good quality at great prices with quick delivery times (ikea.co.uk). Made.com sources well-designed modern pieces directly from the makers – saving you costs. Try Dunelm for inexpensive but chic smaller buys such as bathroom mirrors (dunelm.com).

Second-hand furniture. Antiques can be great value: they are well made from solid wood, lasting far longer than flat-pack, yet often costing less. Sunbury antiques market (sunburyantiques.com), in southwest London, is a trade secret, or find a market near you at iacf.co.uk. Search eBay.co.uk with product names to save on specific brands, or try council- and charity-run furniture re-use projects (frn.org.uk). But don't buy any old junk – if you're not prepared to live with it, your tenants probably won't be either. Save on transport by booking shared space in a courier's van via AnyVan.com.

Ten ways to up your property's appeal

To achieve the highest possible rent and attract the best tenants, you need to **reduce barriers** – tackle any issues that will deter tenants – and **make it attractive** by taking positive steps to style the property.

It can be hard to see the faults in your own property, especially if you've lived there and are used to the funny smells and décor. Ask an honest friend or good agent to point out any barriers that might put off tenants. An avocado bathroom suite or tired kitchen might need a refurb (page along swiftly to Chapter 16 'Make the improvements that matter' for more on this). However, many problems are far simpler to fix.

Eleven full bin bags stuffed up flat's appeal

Here's how not to dress for lettings success. Swift once took on a rental property laden with half-melted candles, 17 vases, piles of pink cushions, two old sleeping bags and a fondue set – some left by the owner in the hope that they'd be of use, then successive strata of nick-nacks were added by tenants, until all the storage in the flat was full. It had snowballed to the point where Swift had to remove 11 bin bags of paraphernalia that only served to narrow the flat's appeal.

Unless you want to target a narrow market (hoarders with a taste for mini Eiffel towers, say), remove all such trinkets and leave the property neutral but not bland.

Here are 10 ways to attract the widest possible selection of tenants:

1. **Clean properly**. People have different cleaning standards but most will mind grubby basins and mouldy walls.
2. **Fix the obvious snags**. Those long-forgotten picture holes in the wall and the sofa used as the cat's scratching post make the whole property look scrappy.
3. **Wipe the front door clean** – first impressions and all that. Have the windows washed, too, for instant sparkle.

4. **Put away any bins that stand in front of the property**. Pick up litter and pull up weeds on the pavement directly outside the entrance. If there is a communal entrance, vacuum it and whisk away the piles of old pizza flyers.

5. **Do the gardening.** A quick garden tidy-up will help communicate that the property is looked after. Pressure-hose the patios to make them look like new.

6. **Put mattress protectors on all the beds**. This will hide any stains and prevent further damage. Ideally dress the beds with linen, duvets, pillows and maybe even a throw.

7. **Stage the property.** If the flat is empty, hang colourful artwork temporarily on existing picture hooks in strategic places. Simply borrow a few pictures from your own home to do this, along with some cushions and lamps for atmosphere.

8. **Free up space.** If you do still live there, keep bulky items like pushchairs and golf clubs in the car for the time being.

9. **Declutter.** Banish toys, stacks of old magazines and the hoard of shoes and coats by the front door to stylish storage boxes, crates under beds and baskets on top of wardrobes.

10. **Clear the kitchen worktops.** Remove kitchen items that you don't use every day, such as the bread machine, food processor and ice-cream maker, and store them.

You may not be able to do all of the above if you have tenants in the property, but do what you can.

With your property now looking its best after you've ticked all the boxes above, you're ready to market it with maximum appeal. Voids, be gone!

The phone call that saved us thousands

After buying our Maida Hill flat with its sash windows and ornate high ceilings, we thought we'd have to kit it out in full with high-end furniture to attract the right tenant. However, one phone call to a local letting agent saved us a fortune: the busy young professionals whom we were targeting would be just as happy with a few basics from Ikea's better ranges.

To make the flat stand out from its competition, we bought a few unique pieces – including a giant Victorian mantelpiece mirror for £50 – at an antiques market, mixing them with Ikea beds. For marketing photos and viewings, we also dressed the flat with artwork, cushions, bed linen and throws borrowed from our own home. The result? A young professional couple immediately took the flat, at the top end of the rent it had been valued for.

Market your property efficiently

How did we ever manage to find homes before the internet? These days more than 90% of property searches start online, and two-thirds of them are via mobile devices, says Zoopla. Local lettings agents, once the first port of call, are no longer the gate-keepers linking tenants and landlords. Nowadays tenants can even do virtual viewings.

Britain's main property portals are Rightmove, Zoopla and OnTheMarket. You cannot list directly on these portals but can access them via online agents (see Chapter 5 'Do you need an agent?'). Whether you use this route or a high-street agent, ensure that your property is on two of the big portals. You can also list for free on websites such as gumtree.com, but Swift has stopped using this after the quality of applicants dropped.

Just being on the right websites is not enough. Make your advert stand out by a mile with:

- Professional photos
- A floorplan
- Well-written copy

Get ahead with professional photos

Isn't it amazing that 1p screws and 18p bananas are advertised with professional photos, but properties worth hundreds of thousands of pounds will be snapped on a lazy estate agent's smartphone, complete with a pig sleeping in the corner, a toilet in a boiler cupboard or what looks suspiciously like a trail of blood all across the garage floor? (See terriblerealestateagentphotos.com for these and other real-life shockers.)

The right photographs can bring your home to life. At £50–£125 for a set, engage a professional photographer if you can. Not only will they get the best shots, they will also edit them to make sure the sky is blue, rooms are bright and frames cropped correctly. By investing in a set of excellent photos before you start renting out your property, you can keep them on file to re-use every time you advertise in future.

Failing that, use a digital SLR camera with a wide-angle lens and a flashgun to shoot as much of each room as possible. One or two 'lifestyle' images of the Aga or the bistro set in the garden can work well, too, but don't overdo it. Move aside cars and bins in front of the house, put away the laundry and wait for the sun to be at the right angle to show off your property to best effect. Shoot when the house is still furnished; empty properties don't photograph well.

What if there are tenants in the property? Such photos are not ideal but you may have no choice. Always arrange with them first, but ask to go when they are out. This will allow you to move any dirty dishes, drying laundry and personal photographs out of the picture to protect their privacy and avoid clutter. You could even add a few homely touches of your own. Take a photo before you move things around (within limits) to ensure you return them to the right places. Also, once the tenancy is over and before the next one starts, return to take a new set of photos that you can keep for future use. That said, some tenants' décor is so tasteful that you might be far better off shooting with it in place than without.

Make sure the best photo – usually the living room (for flats) or the exterior – is the main image on the property portal. If your flat's best feature is its view over a private garden square, don't let the galley kitchen facing the fire escape be the first thing that online users see.

Save time with floorplans

Historically floorplans have been used to market higher-end rentals but they are becoming more common – for good reason: they're an invaluable marketing tool for all properties. Floorplans only need to be done once, but can help a would-be tenant work out whether the property is right for them or not, saving both your time and theirs. A professional photographer or the assessor who does your energy performance certificate can usually create a floorplan for £20–£30 extra if they're visiting anyway.

Your aim when marketing a property is not only to paint a picture of a lovely home, but also to give as many facts as possible so that prospective tenants can make an informed decision to view. That means you will only attract those likely to take it.

Write like a human (not an estate agent)

Legend tells of one estate agent who described a driveway as a 'multi-vehicular block paviour parking facility'. That is not the sort of description you want in your advert. Edit out the syrup (see jargon buster), but make sure you include everything a tenant really wants to know:

- **Where?** State not only the area (and don't call it central Manchester when it's actually Salford Quays), but also how far it is in distance – not minutes – from transport, shops, restaurants and parks.

- **What?** Is it a flat? Terraced house? Detached? People like to know these things. How many bedrooms are there, and how big? It's not a double if fitting in the world's smallest double bed means you can't open the door. Mention whether it's furnished or not. Highlight any pluses, such as private parking, a separate entrance, wooden floors, exposed beams or high ceilings. And say if it has a shower, as people like us won't bite if it lacks one. (But please don't say it 'benefits from a bath fitted within and a shower-mixer unit'. Spare us.)
- **When?** From which date is it available?
- **Who?** Specify your tenant preference, for example 'no students or housing benefit'. 'Deposit and references required' will discourage those on an income too low for the rent. Even better, appeal directly to your ideal tenant with a phrase like 'to suit couple/three sharers'.
- **How much?** To attract the most (and best) applicants, you need to get your asking rent just right. Set it £10 or so below the going rate you've worked out by using the valuation process we described in Chapter 2 'Run your numbers', and the phone will soon be ringing. But get the rent wrong and it will stay silent, with all your hard work being for nowt.

Telling the world that your property is 'spectacular' doesn't mean anything. Rather, show why it's so spectacular:

> **2 bed flat to rent | £3,000 pcm (£692 pw)**
>
> Trebovir Road, Earls Court, London SW5
>
> This two-bedroom penthouse with a private lift, on the fifth floor of a stucco-fronted terrace in the heart of Earls Court, has an L-shaped open-plan kitchen/dining/living room offering great views through 6ft windows on two sides. Off the living area is a sizeable private roof terrace, landscaped with mature container plants.

Both bedrooms are spacious doubles with built-in wardrobes and dark wooden floors; both bathrooms have showers, one of them walk-in. On a quiet side road, the flat is 400yd from Earls Court Tube station (District and Piccadilly lines) and its surrounding delis, shops and restaurants.

Available furnished or unfurnished from March 1. To suit a professional couple or two sharers; deposit and references required.

Jargon buster

Chelsea (replace area name as appropriate) West: the dodgy bit just west of the posh bit.

Compact: you can cook dinner while showering.

Community feel: curtain-twitcher lives across the road.

Convenient location: above a kebab shop.

Deceptively spacious: you've been deceived if you think this is spacious.

Excellent transport links: next to the M25.

Garden flat: damp, dark hovel in the basement.

Immaculately presented: no kids, no stuff, no life. If you move in, it won't look like that.

Low-maintenance courtyard garden: concrete postage stamp prone to weeds.

Within easy reach of local schools: you'll be picking the yoofs' empty crisp packets out of the privet after every lunch break.

What if my home is not letting?

If your house is the bricks-and-mortar equivalent of Desperate Dolores in the lonely hearts column, that's the reason for it. Don't wait for your agent to contact you, but find out what feedback they get from viewings. Either the asking rent is too high (painful as it is, lower it decisively – having to foot 5% of your monthly mortgage payment is still better than 100% of it), or Dolores might need a makeover. Tenants only ever want bright and light. Act on what they say: don't let an unkempt lawn or a peeling bathroom floor scupper Dolores's future happiness.

Two other factors might be at work:

Soft criteria. These are your preferences on tenant types, letting furnished (or not), allowing pets, and so on. The narrower your brief is ('single Aquarius with cat'), the smaller your pool of potential tenants becomes – and the longer your property will take to let. Don't insist on leaving your furniture if all the applicants are families who want to bring their own. Being more flexible will help.

Hard criteria. If your flat is on the fourth floor with no lift, only available for six months or in an area with low demand, it will be harder to let. There's not much you can do about that.

With your property shipshape, you're now all set to meet Mr and Mrs Right (or at least, Mr and Mrs Distinct Possibility). But before we look at how to pick and keep your dream tenants in the 'People' section, there are still a few technical hoops to jump through in the next chapter. Onwards!

CHAPTER 7

Tick the legal boxes

In this chapter:

- **Gas, fire and electrics: the serious stuff you have to do to keep your tenants safe, your insurance valid and yourself out of jail**
- **All you need to know about energy performance certificates and the rules on being green**
- **Landlord licensing and HMOs made simple (which is no easy task).**

Gas safety checks, electrical tests, smoke detectors... Before you roll your eyes at the miles of red tape landlords have to disentangle, here is why it's necessary:

The £250 fire door that cost five lives

A young couple, their baby son and their young niece and nephew all burnt to death trapped in their first-floor flat in Prestatyn, north Wales, because there was no fire door to slow the flames. Their neighbour had set alight their pushchair in the communal hallway because she was fed up with it being left outside her flat. The fire blazed up the stairs, which acted like a chimney in the absence of a fire door, with such intense heat that it melted the TV and the cooker hood.

The fire brigade – which happened to include Jay Liptrot, owner of the flat – arrived six minutes after the 999 call. Liptrot fought desperately to save his tenants, but it was already too late.

In the subsequent court case in 2015, Liptrot was jailed for 15 months and lost his job after pleading guilty to failing to take fire precautions, exposing people to risk. A £250 fire door off the hallway, instead of the flimsy glass and wood front door, would have slowed the inferno for 30 minutes, saving the family's lives. The neighbour who started the fire, Melanie Smith, 43, was jailed for 30 years.

Far worse, though, was the human cost. The 29-year-old mother of Skye, 2, and Bailey, 4, who perished on what was meant to be a sleepover with their cousin Charlie, 15 months, said: 'When I wake up in the morning, that first minute is beautiful. In those 60 seconds I feel no pain and I'm just listening for the laughter and footsteps running across the landing in the hope that my bedroom door will fly open and they will come bouncing in and jump onto the bed so that I can smother them in kisses. It is then that reality sets in. My heart is wrenched and the heavy empty feeling engulfs me.'

Being a landlord is a serious responsibility. You have to keep your tenants safe, and if you don't, the consequences can be devastating. Not only could you face fines and prison, but you may also have to live with grief like that of Skye and Bailey's mum on your conscience.

So, what are your obligations? Note, the following applies in England, as Scotland and Wales have their own rules.

Safety

Above all, be safe. And safe does not mean what your brother-in-law's builder says is 'all good, luv'. In a moment we'll cover the specific tests you have to do, but your safety responsibilities don't stop there. You have a general duty of care to take all reasonable steps. For example, glazed doors need safety glass, stairs need handrails, and there should be no old lead water pipes or exposed asbestos fibres.

If your tenant complains to the local council, or the council thinks your property is dangerous, officials can force you to fix any 'category one' hazards under the Housing Health and Safety Rating System (HHSRS). The council can also fix it themselves and bill you for the cost, or stop you or anyone else from using part or all of the property.

But perhaps more relevant (you're reading this book, so you're probably not a criminal landlord who expects your tenants to freeze in a sub-zero shed) is the fact that *your insurance will likely be invalid if you break the rules.*

Plus, you're leaving yourself open to a civil claim for damages if, say, a tenant falls down the stairs because he tripped on the loose carpet or there was no rail.

Gas safety certificate

Annually, **£65–£125.**

Gas leaks can kill through carbon monoxide poisoning or explosions. That's why, by law, you have to maintain gas pipework, flues and appliances in a safe condition.

An engineer on the Gas Safe register has to test the gas supply and all gas appliances in your rented property once a year. Not doing so can land you with an unlimited fine, prison sentence or – if someone dies – manslaughter charges.

All gas equipment has to be fitted by a Gas Safe engineer. (Find one at gassaferegister.co.uk.) Unfortunately there is no national register of certificates, so you will need to check your own records to see if you have a valid one and keep track of the annual renewal dates yourself.

You have to give your tenants a copy of this certificate when they move in, and again within 28 days after each annual test. If you don't, you lose your right to end the tenancy without giving a reason.

Smoke and carbon monoxide alarms

At the start of each tenancy, **£15–£25 per alarm.**

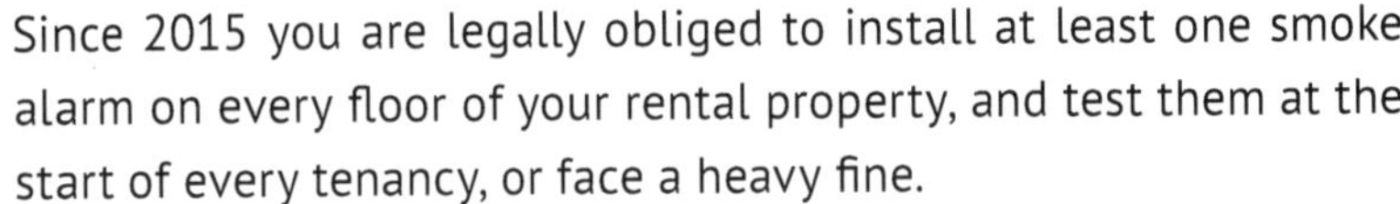

Since 2015 you are legally obliged to install at least one smoke alarm on every floor of your rental property, and test them at the start of every tenancy, or face a heavy fine.

You have to fit carbon monoxide alarms in every room with a solid fuel appliance, such as a coal fire or wood burning stove. To be prudent, also place them in rooms with gas appliances, such as a boiler, gas cooker or gas fireplace.

After your initial check, your tenants are responsible for testing the alarms during the tenancy, ideally once a month.

Landlord jailed over broken smoke alarms

Something doesn't necessarily have to go wrong for poor safety measures to get you into trouble. In 2015 Ishaq Hussein, an experienced landlord, got four months in prison after fire safety inspectors found he had left his Reading tenants without working smoke detectors for two years. Also, a washing machine blocked the escape route, there was no firefighting equipment and the upstairs carpet was a trip hazard.

That said, replacing your old smoke alarms can land you in trouble, too – at least with the neighbours. On their first night in their new rented home, friends were kept up by shrill beeping. It was piercing enough to wake three different neighbours, one of whom left an angry note on the door. Another finally called the fire brigade, who found about 40 faulty smoke alarms left by the landlord in the rubbish bags outside the house.

Fire safety

From £10, at the start of letting; every two to three years for blocks of flats.

By law, all upholstered furniture, beds, mattresses and nursery furniture must have fire safety labels.

You have a duty to take general fire precautions, for example:

- The escape route must be clear: your tenants shouldn't need a key to open the front door from inside, and some second-floor bedroom windows should open wide enough to jump out
- Don't have something combustible right next to an ignition source, like a boiler above the hob
- It's a good idea to supply a kitemarked fire blanket (£10).

Fire safety can be fiendishly complex. There are no hard and fast rules: each property is unique, and you have to look at it as a whole. The best official guidance (mostly in plain English) is the Lacors Fire Safety Guide – google that for the latest copy.

It gets more complicated if you own a share-of-freehold flat. By law you (or the building's managing agent) must do a fire risk assessment of the common parts every two to three years – that means the shared hallway and stairs of the whole block, even if it's a Victorian terrace converted into only two flats. You can do this written risk assessment yourself (download a free form at safelincs.co.uk) or pay a fire safety officer from around £100. You also have to reduce or remove the risks. All doors to the escape route, including the internal front door to your flat, must be a 30-minute fire door (from around £200). Check yours for official FD30 labels along the sides. If it's less than 44mm thick, it's not a fire door. Keep all passages and stairs out of the building clear of clutter and combustibles, so paint the communal stairway rather than lining it with fabric wallpaper. And don't allow tenants to leave bikes in the hallway.

'It won't burst into flames'

One set of tenants dumped a chest of drawers in the communal hallway for months, despite warnings that they would be charged with the fire hazard's removal costs, 'likely to be in the region of £100–£150 from a private firm'.

The response? 'It's a piece of furniture and I can guarantee that it will not burst into flames. If it goes missing I will report you to the police for theft, and will charge you with the cost of a new one, likely to be in the region of £600–£800 from a private supplier.'

Witty as the answer might be, legally it's wrong.

Electrical safety checks

Every five years, plus annual checks by you, **£120–£200.**

You must ensure all the electrics are safe. So, at the start of every tenancy and annually:

- Visually check sockets, light fittings and switches for broken parts, damaged cables and signs of scorching.
- Ensure all appliances have at least the CE safety mark. Check that their wires, plugs and parts have no visible damage or burn marks.

Despite what some pen pushers will tell you, you don't have to do annual PAT tests on any appliances – and just as well, for at £30 a pop most landlords would rather dump their perfectly serviceable kettles and toasters in silvery Scafell Pikes all over Britain.

By law, an electrician has to test the electrical installation of any property let to three or more sharers every five years (£120–£200). Proposed new rules will probably make this a requirement for all rental homes from 2017.

You also have a legal obligation to use only qualified people to carry out electrical work. Find one at niceic.com, elecsa.co.uk or napit.org.uk.

Legionella risks

Free. At the start of letting; whenever there are changes to your water installation.

What, Legionella? Yup, you've got to do a risk assessment on that one, too, even if you have no clue what Legionella is. It's actually a bacterium found in water that, if inhaled in a fine spray, can cause Legionnaires' Disease – a potentially fatal form of pneumonia.

It breeds in standing water at 20–45C, so if you have water tanks, the cold one should be kept at under 20C. The hot tank should distribute at 50C and heat to 60C for one hour a day – killing the critters. The tanks' lids should also close tightly so no adventurous animals can get in. A combi-boiler means you're probably safe.

Also ensure there are no old pipes to disused appliances where water can stagnate, or attached hosepipes that can backwash into the house's pipework. Let all the taps run a bit before letting out the property after it's been empty for a while. Tell tenants not to adjust the water temperatures. You can get your clipboard out and write down that you've checked all this – there's no need to pay an expert for tests (hse.gov.uk/legionnaires).

Energy efficiency

Energy performance certificate

Every 10 years, **£40–£85.**

So the tenants can see upfront if the heating will cost them a bomb, you are legally obliged to get an energy performance certificate (EPC). You have to arrange the EPC check before you advertise your rental property, and you must include the rating in the advert within seven days. You must also show the certificate at viewings, send it out to anyone who asks for the property's details, and give your tenants a copy before they move in. If you don't, you face a £200 fine and you lose your right to end the tenancy easily.

EPCs have to be done whenever a property is let, built or sold, so there might already be one for your house. Check this on the national EPC database (epcregister.com), from where you can download a free copy – saving you £40–£85 for a new one. Use the same register to find an EPC assessor near you.

An EPC is valid for 10 years if there are no big changes to the property. The property has to be re-rated if you do any major building works or fit double-glazing.

Minimum green standards

Climate change is now more than hot air for landlords. From April 2018, you'll be banned from granting a new tenancy on a home with the lowest two EPC ratings of F and G, unless it's exempt. (If the fixes cost more than they would save on bills over a seven-year period, you're probably exempt. You're also exempt if a surveyor finds the changes will devalue your property by 5% or more, or you need consent for the works from a third party – like your tenant or freeholder – but they refuse.) In practice, F and G ratings are rare, but check on your EPC if you're affected so you can plan ahead to upgrade during tenant changeovers.

Tenants may ask your consent to make improvements funded by grants or by themselves. You're not required to pay for these (unless you want to), but you can't refuse reasonable requests.

We can (mostly) see the point of the laws above, but next up are rules born out of the control freakery of clipboard-bearing numpties.

Landlord licensing schemes

Every five years if it applies in your area, **from £500.**

How do you prevent a tenant from kicking someone's head in? You make his landlord get a licence. Nope, that's not a joke. Reducing 'anti-social behaviour' is the reason why about one in ten councils in England have brought in selective licensing for landlords. In Wales and Scotland, you need a licence to let almost any home.

The schemes are also meant to raise living standards. However, they only require that you do the things any half-baked landlord would do anyway, like have a contract, tenant references, a gas safety certificate, smoke alarms and safe electrics (most of which are already legislated). A slum landlord intent on breaking these laws won't start sticking to them just because he now has to get a licence. He'll just break the licence law, too. Duh!

What's really needed is better enforcement, not more rules. In 2012, there were 150,000 more people prosecuted for not having a TV licence than for poor or criminal property practices. In the meantime, all landlord licensing does is make the government look like they're doing something to help renters trapped by the housing crisis.

However silly, if landlord licensing applies in your area, you'll have to stump up around £500 for a five-year licence *per rental property of any kind*. Check with your council on its rules – fines can be unlimited. You might even have to endure plastic pastries and an approximation of coffee while council stooges wax on about the absolute virtue of their ever-expanding rulebook in a day-long course.

At the time of writing, six London boroughs and around thirty other councils across England were mugging landlords – and if you're not among those, your area might be next. Some schemes cover the whole city or borough (for example, Liverpool and Newham); others only specific streets. Wales and Scotland have countrywide schemes (rentsmart.gov.wales; landlordregistrationscotland.gov.uk). Londonpropertylicensing.co.uk lists the rules for all London boroughs.

Still reading? We're almost done with this thrill-a-minute stuff. Just one more to go...

Houses in multiple occupation (HMOs)

Every five years or fewer, depending on your council, **£300–£1,100.**

When it comes to this sort of regulation, too much is never enough – or at least, that's what the box tickers in grey shoes seem to think.

In 1985 the law defined 'multiple occupation' in two sentences; by 2004 the definition stretched over six pages.

We'll make it as plain as can be. So here goes: an HMO is where three or more people who don't form a single household share a kitchen or bathroom. Common examples are a group of friends sharing a house, a student house, or a house let by room. But – you've guessed it – the plot thickens from there, as rules vary for different types of HMOs (gov.uk/house-in-multiple-occupation-licence):

- **Electrical tests.** As we've seen above, the electrical system of any HMO let to three or more sharers has to be checked by an electrician every five years.
- **Licences.** All HMOs of three or more storeys with five or more sharers need a 'mandatory' licence (from £300). From 2017 proposed laws would extend this to all homes with five or more sharers. Some councils also require 'additional' licences for smaller HMOs with as few as three people. To get a licence, the HMO has to adhere to the council's rules for room sizes, bathroom and kitchen ratios and fire safety.
- **Planning permission.** In England, you always need planning permission for an HMO of seven or more sharers. Many councils, including Oxford and Portsmouth, require the same consent for HMOs of three to six people. Planning looks at the use of the property, while licensing concerns the health and safety of the tenants.

Ask your council for details on what applies in your area. HMO rules for all London boroughs are set out on londonpropertylicensing.co.uk.

Rules are ever tightening to clamp down on 'beds in sheds' where, in one case, 16 tenants had to share a single shower. If you don't comply, you can face jail, unlimited fines and clawback of all rent paid while in breach. Not for amateurs, then.

Why bother with all the hoop jumping? An HMO is a lot of work, but the rent can dwarf what you'll earn from the same house as a single family let. We'll look at the practicalities of running small HMOs let to young professional sharers in Chapter 10 'The dos and don'ts for six tenant types'.

In summary, the golden rule is: if you supply it, make sure it's safe. You don't have to bubble-wrap your tenants or foresee freak accidents, but they shouldn't have to dice with death while living in your property. And even if no one gets hurt, your insurance won't pay out if you break the rules. But hey, if you've persevered through these pages of death, destruction and daft licensing laws, you won't put a foot wrong.

Part 3
People

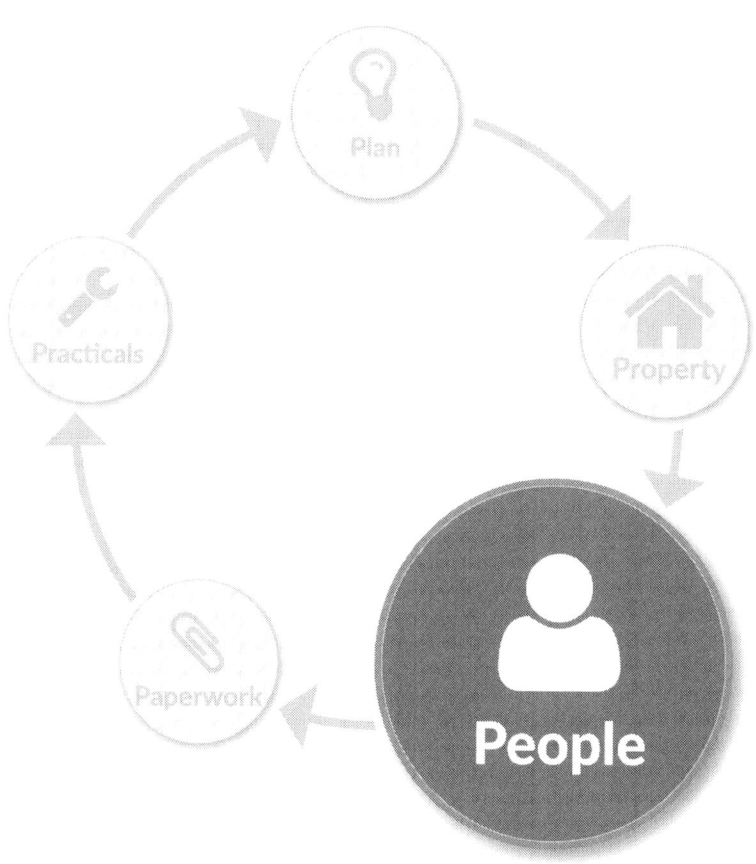

CHAPTER 8

How to find a good tenant

In this chapter:

- **Pointers to help you prepare for viewings like a pro**
- **Questions to screen time wasters and tips on negotiating the best deal**
- **The art and science of choosing trustworthy tenants through gut feeling and thorough checks.**

As the ruler of your new rental empire, you have two enemies of the (e)state: voids and bad tenants. Voids – when your place sits empty while you still have to pay the mortgage month after month – are, well, best avoided. Bad tenants, however, are much worse: getting rid of them can take eight months or more, some £300 in court costs – plus thousands more if the tenant fights the eviction – and many a sleepless night. And that's not counting the property damage, fallout with angry neighbours and mountain of unpaid utility bills you may have to deal with. Bad tenants are very bad indeed.

The strange case of the humps in the night

In a respectable part of central London a clean-cut young man rented a flat from a well-known high street agent. He agreed to pay a premium rent and signed the year-long contract, to the owners' delight. All went well for a month or two, until the downstairs neighbours – and their young children – started being woken up by humps in the night. Then strange men, including a rabbi in full regalia, started ringing the buzzer at all hours asking for a massage. The upstairs flat, it was clear, had been turned into a brothel.

Legal threats and a police raid had no effect. Eleven months and £3,500 in costs later, it finally stopped after the building's freeholder, managed by Daniel, hired a security guard to keep out punters. (Warning: do not try this at home. It's illegal for you to harass your tenants, but in this case the muscle was brought in by the freeholder – not the landlord – upon legal advice. The women working in the flat were not the signed tenants, plus the building's lease banned running a business and 'illegal or immoral activity'.)

Police investigation revealed that the original tenant had a criminal record. Tenants are not always what they seem, and although not fool proof, thorough reference checks are highly advised. And that's putting it politely.

The good news for your defence strategy is that the same tactics take out both voids and bad tenants:

- **Presentation.** The quality of your property is the most important factor. As we've seen earlier, properties attract the tenants they deserve. Preparing your property with needed repairs, the right furnishings and some homely touches (see Chapter 6: 'Prep and promote your property') will make the world of difference.
- **Flexibility.** The more open you are on things such as start dates, tenancy length, pets, furnishing and pre-tenancy works, the greater your chance of finding a good tenant.

Once you get these two points right, you're ready to start booking appointments. In the rest of this section we'll talk you through the finer points of viewings, negotiation and vetting tenants.

Why not to let to friends

Some 'friends of friends' turn out to be your worst enemy. Kevin and Nadia – a colleague of Martina's – had bought and done up a three-bedroom house in Leytonstone, east London, but weren't quite ready to move in themselves. So when a friend of a friend said she'd like to rent it, it seemed like a no-brainer. She was a single mother with twin teenage daughters moving from Germany, claimed to have a job offer and promised a month's deposit and three months' rent upfront – meaning Kevin and Nadia could pay off their builders.

She seemed like someone who would look after the place they'd just done up, but looking back, Nadia can't believe they took her on. 'Neither of us had a good feeling about her and she didn't actually have a job. But for some reason, possibly laziness after several months of renovations, and the thought of not having to advertise the place and show people round, we did.'

Once they had signed the six-month contract, the tenant never paid rent again. Because Kevin and Nadia had forgotten to protect the deposit in time, they lost their automatic right to take their property back at the end of the six-month term. Sixteen months, £25,000 in rent arrears and £4,000 in legal costs later, she was still there and it looked like it would take another eight months before they'd get her out.

'Obviously, the whole thing has been enormously stressful and upsetting,' Nadia says. 'We have both taken on extra work to pay our own rent as well as the mortgage, but have to borrow to pay for legal fees. (Unlike her, we don't get legal aid!) We feel as though we are in limbo. We don't know when we will be able to move in or whether we'll have enough money for holidays.'

Her advice? 'Trust your instincts and never take on a friend, or friend of a friend. But if you do, treat it as seriously as if it were a stranger.'

What about letting to people you know well? That old adage about not mixing business and pleasure is never truer than in lettings: your friends will probably not see the relationship as business. You'll feel bad for charging a deposit or raising the rent, and they won't like you for it either. If you want to stay friends, stay just that. Don't let to them in the first place.

How to screen tenants before viewings

If you plan to do your own viewings, it helps to ask the prospective tenant a few screening questions over the phone before they view. This will not only give you a better feel for the tenant, but it will also save your time and theirs: you can avoid wasted viewings by highlighting any deal breakers early on.

Some good screening questions to ask your prospective tenants are:

- Why are they moving, and why are they interested in viewing your property in particular?
- Are they already familiar with the area or is it completely new to them?
- How long a rental contract are they looking for, and what sort of break clause would they be comfortable with?
- Are they sharers, a couple or a family unit? Will there be children living at the property?
- What kind of job stability do they have?
- Do they earn sufficiently to cover the rent themselves? Do they receive benefits, or help from a guarantor?
- Do they have pets? If so, what type of pet? (A goldfish might cause ever so slightly less damage than a pit-bull terrier.)
- Do they smoke?

It's unlikely that you will be able to cover all these points in your initial conversation, but you can at least ask the ones that are most important to you and then leave any remaining questions for the viewing. Even this initial conversation can give you a good gut feeling for the type of tenant they might be.

If there is something obvious about the location that could put tenants off, for example, if it's far from public transport, it sometimes helps to set their expectations with a light remark. However, if the flat is lovely inside yet there's a power station next door, you're better off saying nothing and leaving them to weigh up the pros and cons for themselves.

How to do viewings like a pro

Now that you have those professional couples and sharers lining up for your penthouse, bunch viewings together to create a buzz. If one set of applicants brushes past another on their way in or out, they'll know a cheeky offer won't cut it.

Scheduling viewings in clusters will also save you time. In Daniel's experience, one in ten people won't turn up and won't bother letting you know – even after you've confirmed the appointment by text on the day (which is advisable to do to avoid even more no-shows).

The woman in the wardrobe

You never quite know what you'll find on a viewing. When Daniel first arrived in London more than 20 years ago, he went to see a four-bedroom split-level flat he intended to share with friends. The agent led them inside and showed them the downstairs living areas and kitchen. About five minutes into the viewing, a handyman came downstairs – much to the surprise of the agent, who was unaware of his presence in the property. A few minutes later, while viewing one of the bedrooms upstairs, Daniel opened a built-in wardrobe to find a (fully-clothed) woman hiding inside.

'Shhhh,' she whispered, putting her finger to her pursed lips. One can only wonder what the two of them were up to.

Even if you are quite sure tenants are out during a viewing, do knock and wait a good minute or two before entering.

Small things make a big difference to showing your property in the best light. Try the following directly before a viewing:

- Open all curtains and blinds fully to maximise natural light
- Switch on all lights at night; ditto on a dull day or in rooms with little sunlight
- Open the windows to air the property well
- Switch on the heating if it's cold. You don't want your visitors to shiver through the viewing
- Make the beds – an unmade bed really makes a room look untidy
- Discreetly hide drying laundry or clothes lying on the floor. (Under the duvet makes a great emergency hideout)
- Hang towels tidily in the bathrooms
- If it's your own home and you are still living there, an open fire and soft music won't seem like overkill. You're just relaxing after a long day, right?

How to do viewings with tenants in situ

Include a clause in your contract to allow viewings in the final two months. Try to schedule them for when the tenants are out, always give tenants at least 24 hours' notice, and take the correct key (unlike one agent from a certain chain who broke in to do a viewing, changed the locks and failed to give the tenants a new key).

If the tenants are very messy, arrive early to tidy up without being too intrusive. Just remember to mess everything up again before you leave – taking a photo beforehand helps. You could offer the tenants a cash bonus if they keep things spick and span and the flat is let with less than a week's void. For a real pigsty, though, you might have to wait until they've left.

Besides taking the right key, it's also helpful to have the key facts to hand. This may sound obvious but you'd be surprised at how often agents come up blank. Better still, hand a printout to prospective tenants to mull over. This will also avoid misunderstandings. Key facts include:

- The rent expressed both per week and per month (that's 4.33 times the weekly rate)
- The exact date when the property becomes available
- Tenancy length and whether there's a break clause
- Very importantly, exactly what furniture will be provided. This can cause whole deals to fall through
- The annual council tax; water bill and whether this is metered; the average monthly gas and electricity bills
- A copy of the energy performance certificate. (By law you have to give this to prospective tenants, as explained in the previous chapter)
- What deposit and fees are payable to the agent and inventory clerk. All costs should be clear
- Which way the property faces and how much direct sunlight it gets as a result
- Where the nearest shops, pubs and restaurants are
- Whether the nearby schools are good and what age ranges they cater for
- The nearest transport links, including the distance there, the frequency and journey times
- Whether parking is available and if there are any restrictions
- Any other restrictions, for example on pets, or tenant obligations, such as maintaining the garden.

Let the tenants enter rooms first so you don't take up space and make it feel cramped. If you're a woman doing a viewing alone, it's safer to be the person closest to the exit. Prop the front door open just to be sure.

The art of negotiation in lettings

To achieve the highest possible rent, good negotiation is key. Here knowledge truly is power: the best lettings negotiators give nothing away while trying to establish as many key facts from the tenant as possible.

Don't reveal any of your main drivers. Where an agent is letting your property, don't disclose any personal facts to them – they may not be able to resist whispering them to the tenant. If you conduct your own viewings, don't volunteer any information on yourself. Letting it slip that you are moving countries in a month (and are desperate to find a tenant who will move in straight away to help cover your many costs) will not help your cause.

Some of the facts to glean from prospective tenants are:

- How sold they are on your particular property judging by their body language and conversation: talking about where their furniture would fit indicates a strong like, while asking if you have any other similar properties for rent reveals ambivalence or dislike
- What time pressure they are under and how long it is before they have to move
- How many similar properties they've seen, to gauge your competition. A disarming question helps, such as: 'You are the experts on two-bedroom flats in this area right now. How does this one compare?'
- If they seem quite price sensitive or if it's more about finding the right property
- Whether they are clear on the location they want. If not, they are time wasters
- If there is a particular sticking point for them. If so, leverage this as a point of negotiation.

As a landlord, you need to decide what are your non-negotiables. The primary non-negotiable is to find the right type of tenant for your property. But be realistic: the shoe should fit – a top lawyer is unlikely to take your ex-council flat. Overall, the highest rent is secondary to the right tenant, as the wrong tenant can cost you a lot more.

Apart from these non-negotiables, on what are you prepared to back down? Consider:

- Do you have strong preferences on the number of tenants? Children? Pets? Smoking? Try not to be too descriptive
- Is the rental level critical to you: do you have a mortgage payment or other cost to cover?
- Are the contract length and break clause timing important to you? Are you working within a fixed window?
- Are you prepared to spend any money on furniture or tenant requests?

Good negotiation is about give and take. Ideally you want to give in on issues that are important to the tenant but less so to you, without compromising on your own non-negotiables.

Teaspoons seal the deal

Here's how to find a happy medium. Media salesman Rupert and PR manager Joanne, both in their late twenties, were a perfect fit for their north London landlord, even offering close to the asking rent. However, they could only move in a month after the two-bedroom flat became vacant, which would have meant a £1,900 void period. They also had very few belongings, so asked for a new mattress, a second double bed plus a fully equipped kitchen – down to the teaspoons. The owner agreed to their requests, on condition that they move in three weeks earlier. Buying all they asked for came to less than £800, leaving the owner £700 better off than he'd have been with the full month's void. And he had his ideal tenants.

How to vet tenants thoroughly

The importance of gut feeling

The truism that leopards don't change their spots is all too apt in lettings: the impression that prospective tenants give when you first meet them is likely to be how they'll continue to behave once they live in your house. Though you can't judge by appearance, their behaviour can tell you a lot. Small things like arriving on time and respecting you as a landlord can indicate their attitude towards the rental.

If they keep changing their mind, make lots of demands or ask for special treatment – for example, if they want to reserve the flat without paying a holding deposit – it spells trouble. You'll be better off risking a void until you find the right tenant than going with Mr Tricky just because you have no other options.

Gut feeling won't show up on any reference checks and is a big plus of doing viewings yourself. If you use an agent, ask them for their first impressions of any prospective tenant: would they let to them if it were their own property? It's not the only factor to consider – you still need to check that they earn enough, but gut feeling is often an underestimated ingredient in choosing tenants.

What a reference check is, isn't and should be

Even if you have a good feeling about tenants, don't skip doing a thorough reference check on each person. This is one of the most important steps for you as a landlord – remember that brothel flat? Beware the sharply dressed charlatans who absolutely *have* to move in this very day, with promises of above-asking rent but no time for checks or deposits. They seem too good to be true because that's exactly what they are.

If you use an agent, check what they check. Ask them to send you the results of the reference check. You are entitled to see this under data protection law, as long as the agent made it clear to the tenant and referee that this would happen.

Most agents use a referencing company to do the checks, usually paid for by the tenants as a non-refundable fee. If you self-manage, you can do the same: for £20–£30 these companies will do the legwork for you, saving you hours of phoning around. Search 'tenant referencing' to find a provider.

So what should be included? The purpose of a reference check is to confirm that the tenants are who they say they are, that they can afford the rent and that they have honoured past commitments.

Nevertheless, it's *not* a character check. Good references won't guarantee that they will make good tenants. They are not fool proof: some tenants have been known to play the system with false employers and accommodation references. Plus previous evictions won't even show up on a reference check unless the landlord pushed it all the way to a county court judgement for unpaid rent. Now there's a sobering thought.

A standard reference check should include:

- **Employment reference.** Details of the employer, job title, salary, how long the tenant has worked there and that they are not under notice to leave. The referencing company (or you) need to double-check this: call the employer's switchboard, check the tenant's job title and ask to be put through. That way you'll know if he got his mate Gary to vouch for him.
- **Landlord reference.** The start and end date of the tenants' current tenancy, the rent, whether it was paid on time and their conduct as tenants. Again, call the landlord to double-check. They might be nervous to give negative feedback in writing, but more open over the phone.
- **Proof of address.** Current and previous addresses verified with utility bills, bank statements and the voters' roll.
- **Credit report.** Most importantly, this checks for bankruptcy and County Court Judgements (CCJs) – that is unpaid debts. (If the tenant has any, they should tell you before the reference check. There might be a good reason, for example a business failure. Weigh this up against all the other information.) The report also flags up if they are in serious debt

or have a history of missed payments. However, people like students or those who are new to Britain will have a low score simply because there is almost nothing on their credit report. This is not necessarily a bad thing, but you may then want extra evidence.

- **Bank account check** – that they have a valid UK bank account.
- **Right to Rent check** – that they have the right to live and work in the UK (more about this shortly).

Based on all this, the reference report will suggest a maximum affordable rent of 25–35% of the tenant's gross income.

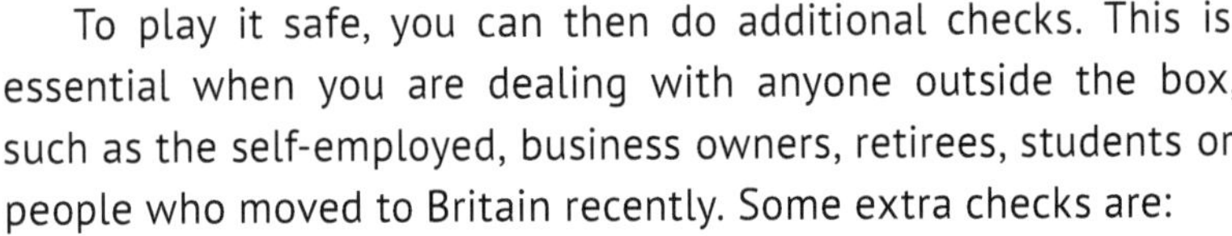

To play it safe, you can then do additional checks. This is essential when you are dealing with anyone outside the box, such as the self-employed, business owners, retirees, students or people who moved to Britain recently. Some extra checks are:

- Search for them on Google or LinkedIn to verify their employment. This is a great way to cross-reference anything they've said in passing. If things don't add up, gently prod the tenants for answers. And if they can't explain it, don't let to them
- If they are self-employed or have their own company, ask for six months' bank statements or two years' accounts
- Get a reference from the landlord *before the last one*, as their current landlord might say anything to get rid of terrible tenants. Also, check the Land Registry for whether the named landlord actually owns the property rented by the tenant (£3, eservices.landregistry.gov.uk).

The clearer the picture, the better. However, if you've done all this and there is still insufficient evidence that the rent will be paid, there are two further options. Ask for all or some of the rent to be paid in advance. But be suspicious of willy-nilly offers of six months' rent upfront – that's a classic ruse to set up cannabis farms. Some serial defaulters also offer generous advances, but then refuse to pay any more once they're in the property.

Have a working homeowner (for instance, a student's parents) guarantee the tenancy, or play it even safer with two guarantors. Do all the reference checks listed above on the guarantor(s) as well.

Still in doubt? Then don't let to them. Your property is one of your biggest assets – it's not worth risking it on people you can't trust. That said, 98% of tenants are honest. The cheats and con-artists make up a small fraction and, if you do everything listed above, they'll look elsewhere for an easier target.

Yuck! Why a bad tenant quite literally stinks

Viewing the shoebox studio that was to become her first buy-to-let, Martina got an inkling of just how much a bad tenant stinks. She gagged at the stench as the agent opened the door: the bedding was soiled, the sink caked in bodily fluids, and inside the bar fridge an unidentifiable object – a decomposing potato, she hoped, not something worse – floating in a sea of grey sludge. The previous tenant had been a drug addict who trashed the place.

An Ikea makeover got rid of all that, but the subsequent tenant did once leave the window open before going on a four-week trip. On his return, a pigeon and its eggs had to be evicted from his bed – but thankfully, no addicts.

Right to Rent checks

Blame the migrant crisis in Europe, but landlords are now on the frontline of this fight. Since 2015, new laws require you to check that tenants have the right to live in Britain before letting a property to them – or face a penalty of up to £3,000 per adult illegal immigrant living there, even if they are not named in the lease.

Lettings agents usually do these checks as part of their standard referencing, but double check that they are done since you have ultimate responsibility. To avoid discrimination, you must check all tenants, including those who seem British. You (or your agent) have to check their original papers with them present, make copies and record the date (gov.uk/check-tenant-right-to-rent-documents). If their permission to stay is limited, you need to do further checks before it runs out.

Is meeting your tenant a good idea?

Meeting your tenants can put your mind to rest. When Catherine, one of Swift's clients, let her one-bedroom flat for the first time, she didn't want to let to just anyone. This was the bay-windowed picture-railed home that she had saved up for, had painted in cosy shades of claret and lime, and had decorated with velvet accent chairs and quirky finds. Seeing her tenant in person, a single professional woman like herself, made all the difference.

However, be wary of scaring tenants off: like you, they are protective of their privacy and an over-zealous landlord is all too much. They want a place to live, not a new best friend.

So, you've done your screened viewings? You've negotiated a win-win deal? And you've vetted your tenants through gut feeling, thorough referencing and Right to Rent checks? Tick, tick, tick? Now you just have to keep them and you'll be safe as houses. In the next chapter, we'll tell you how.

They also demanded to be put up in a hotel after the pesticide was sprayed, despite experts confirming that it would be safe within four hours. Gail drew the line at this but agreed to pay if any clothes were damaged. None were, as the female moths could not fly and were hence unlikely to lay eggs on clothes in wardrobes. She'd been right to put her foot down.

Owners, too, can cross the line when they try to be too involved. An inspection report that says a property is dirty doesn't entitle you to step in until the end of the tenancy – unless the mess is causing damage. Nor can you refuse visitors (see anecdote below), keep disturbing the tenant or change the locks. By law, you must arrange visits at least 24 hours in advance, even for viewings or when sending tradesmen, unless there is an emergency that needs an immediate fix and waiting too long will cause further damage.

It comes down to the basics of tenancy law:

- A tenant has a duty to pay prompt rent and look after their temporary home, with a right to enjoy it freely
- A landlord has a duty to provide a safe home and make prompt repairs, and leave the tenant to enjoy it freely.

Prying neighbour reports 'strange' visits

One landlord asked Swift to interrogate his tenants about a strange man who visited them every Saturday. When Daniel quizzed the landlord further, it turned out that a nosy neighbour had reported the 'most unusual' visits by someone who might well have been the tenants' friend, relative or music teacher. There were no signs that the tenants were doing anything wrong, so Daniel politely refused to investigate. Doing so would have breached the tenants' right to quiet enjoyment of their home.

Collect the rent on the dot

Call us heartless ogres, but rent collection is one area in which not to be soft. You keep your end of the bargain, the tenants keep theirs. Tenants should pay on time, every time – unless there is genuine hardship, which happens in only about 2% of lets. Let things slip, and slack or scatty souls will end up paying later and later.

Require tenants to set up a standing order so the rent reaches your account on the first of every month (though ensure your mortgage goes off a few days later, just to be safe). Check your bank account on the first and call or email your tenant before noon if they haven't paid. They should get the message loud and clear that late payments are not acceptable, which nips bad habits in the bud. Swift's tenants get an email by 9am if they've skipped a payment – and because of that, the agency has never had unpaid rent.

Also report any missed payments immediately to your rent guarantee insurer, in line with their terms. Of course, anyone can fall on hard times, and then you need to be understanding – up to a point. (More on that, and evictions, in Chapter 13 'When things go wrong'.)

Communicate, communicate, communicate

Poor communication is the main reason why tenant relations break down. To avoid that, stick to these principles (we'll keep the sermon short, promise):

- **Be responsive.** If a tenant doesn't feel heard, they're less likely to care for your home and more likely to leave. You don't have to say yes to each and every request, but you do need to acknowledge it and give an answer – which might be a prompt 'no, because...' Ignoring the issue will fan the flames, not let them peter out.
- **Be clear.** Set out all the facts, without emotion or ambiguity. Be honest on timescales. Tell tenants if the boiler will take a week to be replaced in the middle of winter; it's the *not* knowing that makes things worse.

- **Be professional.** Never get personal. Treat your tenants with respect, even if they don't show it to you. That defuses tension.

Communication shreds tenants' macerator fury

When the macerator, which shredded loo waste and controlled the shower outlet, broke for the third time in Joe's southwest London maisonette, his tenants were irate. Yet again their only toilet and shower were out of order, forcing them to use the loo at a nearby Costa coffee shop and wash their hair in the kitchen sink. (Macerators, incidentally, are a very bad idea. Daniel has yet to meet one that hasn't broken down – and he's seen plenty.)

One supplier said the macerator had to be replaced, but there would be a four-day wait for parts. Swift updated the tenants and prepared to put them up in a nearby hotel, defusing their anger. A second supplier managed to fix the macerator the next day, saving Joe more than £1,000 and solving the (now delighted) tenants' loo woes.

Aside from the principles of communication, there's the logistics of it. Daniel encourages Swift's tenants to use email as far as possible. Besides creating a paper trail, landlords can forward all the details to their tradesmen. It also doesn't interrupt anyone's day.

When a tenant is really upset, ring them rather than email. People are less angry on the phone than behind a keyboard. This will make them feel heard. If they are unreasonable and abusive, though, communicate only by factual, unemotional email so everything is in writing. High-maintenance tenants, too, are best dealt with by email. Set boundaries and don't let them abuse your kindness.

Give all tenants a number to call in an emergency, but don't answer calls after hours. Pick up once at 11pm, and you'll get called at all hours about non-emergencies. Do, however, check your voicemail as soon as they've rung so you can respond if water is gushing from the ceiling.

Emergencies aren't always for repairs, either. Daniel once needed to buy a 13ft ladder to rescue a frantic toddler who'd trapped herself alone in a second-floor room.

For a bigger rental portfolio, it might be worth getting a separate number – you can set one up on Skype – or a professional call-answering service that charges by call, not by subscription, from around £1 a call (search 'call-answering service').

Raise the rent without ruffles

Rents have risen faster than inflation over the past decade, so some landlords are used to a 5–10% increase each year. Blanket headlines on soaring rents don't temper their expectations.

The truth is, you can't put up the rent at will. For starters, there are laws around when you can do this (more on that in a moment). Also, weigh up whether you need to raise it at all. If your tenant decides to leave, you'll have costs to find a new one and the risk of an empty period. Even a week or two's void can cancel out any rent increase. Consider, too, how well your current tenants have looked after your flat. A hellish tenant at a higher rate will cost you more than keeping good ones at a lower rent.

By how much could you raise it? The time of year (there's high demand in spring and autumn, but not over Christmas and summer holidays), the local market's performance and the availability of similar properties will all affect what you can charge. These factors are why media reports of general rent hikes can be misleading.

As for when and how you can increase the rent, here's what the law says and what we'd advise:

- **During a tenancy.** Legally, rent is fixed for the whole tenancy term. It can only go up if both parties agree, or if your contract permits it – for example, you can build in a clause allowing an inflation-linked increase once a year. Otherwise you have to wait until the fixed term ends.

- **On renewal.** This is the best time to re-negotiate. It can help to leave some room to come down from your initial proposal. Swift gives tenants two to three months' notice of any planned increase, which they can then accept or decline. This gives landlords enough time to discuss it with tenants and, if they decide to leave, find new tenants.
- **If the tenancy has gone periodic.** If you've left the tenancy rolling after the fixed term's end, you can usually only raise the rent once a year. By law, you have to give the tenants at least a month's notice, though again we'd suggest two to three months. The easiest way to do this is to all agree and sign a written record of that. Or you can send the tenants the right form (a 'Landlord's notice proposing a new rent', from gov.uk/renting-out-a-property/rent-increases). If they object, they can whack you with their own legal notice. Then you can fight it out at the First-Tier Tribunal, which is rare.
- **If the tenancy ends early.** 'Surrender' is when the tenant wants to leave before the end of the fixed term, but is still liable for the rent until the property is re-let. Our advice is to re-market at the same rent. Asking more can prevent re-letting and would be seen as unfair if the old tenant dragged you to a tribunal.

Dealing with difficult neighbours

Ah, curtain twitchers. Some are just a tad too nosy; others are downright nasty. Don't think that tricky neighbours won't matter to you. They'll come back to bite you if your tenants leave – as one of Daniel's clients found out when the downstairs neighbour railed that 'children should not be allowed upstairs'. Said neighbour complained about the tenants letting their son jump off his bed in the mornings and (shock, horror!) running the washing machine at 8pm, until relations were so fraught that the tenants left.

Bear in mind that, by law, you have to declare any dispute with neighbours when you sell, even if it's been resolved – or face being sued by the buyer. For this reason, if you're planning to sell soon, it might not be worth complaining about neighbours' actions at all.

Think outside the box to solve smaller problems, like a messy front garden that belongs to an uninterested ground-floor neighbour. You could simply tidy it up yourself for an hour or two when re-letting or selling, instead of risking a feud.

To address more serious problems, start by talking to the neighbour in person – *not* by bombarding them with aggressive notes. Take things further only if talking fails. Call the council's environmental health section about noise. If the nightmare neighbour is renting, contact their landlord; if they're in a flat, write to the building's freeholder or their managing agent. Keep records of all letters, emails and phone calls.

When a neighbour claims your tenant is causing a nuisance, investigate first. They could have a hidden agenda or just have got it wrong, like the neighbour who accused tenants in our Wimbledon ex-council flat of smoking cannabis when the real offenders lived nearby. If your tenant is guilty, talk to the neighbours and deal with their concerns. Not offering tea and sympathy now could land you with inflated damage claims in the case of, say, a leak down the line – and nasty lawsuits to boot.

Menacing neighbour cuts tenant's power

Jess, a social worker in her fifties, had endured the grumpy neighbour upstairs banging on the floor and pushing angry notes under her door for alleged noise when she came home alone late after work. One night, however, he switched off the electricity to her whole rented flat on the communal circuit board. Scared now, she called Daniel, her lettings agent. As this was harassment, Daniel lodged a complaint with the police and wrote a stern letter to the neighbour. He was so livid that he turned up at Swift's address, but never bothered Jess again.

The ABC of short lets and room lets

After all that harassment chat, let's nip off to the world's biggest holiday let website – just the ticket to fill your place between tenants. (Or is it?) Then we'll look at lodgers, another stop-gap option if you find yourself needing to rent out part, but not all, of your home.

Should I 'Airbnb' it?

It seems so simple. While your property sits empty between tenants, or perhaps even instead of tenants, you could just Airbnb it to tourists or corporate types – doubling or tripling what you'd earn from a long-term let. That would pay for not only the mortgage, but also for the new bathroom/business start-up/round-the-world trip (delete as appropriate).

If only it was that easy. Short lets through Airbnb – now the world's biggest hotelier, despite not owning a single property – and its rivals, such as HomeAway, Wimdu and Onefinestay, come at a price. For each changeover you'll spend up to a day on fielding emails, keys, sheets, cleaners and loo rolls. And that's not counting the mountain of admin you'll face when doing it for the first time (see info below).

For all that hard work, you can charge more – more being somewhere between a standard long let and what a nearby hotel room might cost. But that has to include all bills and maybe weekly cleaning, plus you'll have voids between stays. The place also has to be fully furnished: a suitcase should be all tenants need to move in. By the time you've paid for all that, your profits might be halved.

Note, too, that short lets are not protected under assured shorthold tenancy law. If guests refuse to leave, you can evict them without a court order, but keep invoices and correspondence to prove the intention was a holiday let.

The long list of short-let admin

Before you start a short let, you have to tick a gazillion boxes:

Get the right insurance. A short let will instantly invalidate your buildings insurance. Get a specialist policy that includes liability cover for no-fee claims if some soul slips in the shower.

Ask your lender's consent. Your mortgage provider will see a short let differently from a normal tenancy.

Inform your leaseholder. Your building's lease might ban short lets.

Tell the neighbours, and listen to their concerns about letting strangers into the building or having wheelie suitcases bumping up the communal stairs every night.

Do safety checks. As with a normal let, you need a valid gas safety certificate, safe electrics, smoke and carbon monoxide detectors and fire safety measures. You also need an energy performance certificate if letting for more than four months.

Check local rules. In London, for example, planning rules ban short-letting for more than 90 days a year.

Prepare keys and a manual. Cut several sets of spare keys and write a house guide with information on appliances, the property's quirks and what to see and do in the area.

Do a professional clean. Empty cupboards, dress beds in clean linen and get the whole place sparkling.

Pay the right tax. You can earn £7,500 a year tax free under the Rent-a-room Scheme, but that only applies if you rent part of the house – not the whole place. It's not the Rent-a-house scheme, natch.

Online short-let specialists can do the grunt work for you, starting from 15%, excluding Airbnb fees and bills for cleaning, insurance and safety checks. (Search for 'Airbnb management' and your location.) Otherwise you can use a high-street lettings agent that does short lets. Their typical clients are companies with employees on secondment or home insurance firms that have to put up locals temporarily.

In short, it earns a lot of money but it's a lot of work. To succeed, the property has to be in an area with high demand, ideally in city centres or business districts.

'Help, I need a lodger!'

Like short lets, lodgers can help you pay the mortgage, save up, live your dream – with companionship as a bonus. And, like short lets, lodgers fall outside normal tenancy law. (It's still a good idea to have a contract, though – more on that in Chapter 11 'Get the contract admin right'.) But unlike a short let of your whole home, a lodger means you can use the Rent-a-room Scheme to pocket £7,500 a year tax free (see Chapter 4 'Think ahead to save a fortune in tax').

Advertise for a lodger on flat-share websites such as Spareroom.co.uk. As with a standard tenancy, you'll have to jump through the following hoops:

- **Inform your mortgage provider.** They're unlikely to object, though.
- **Tell your home insurer.** Do it in writing, or your buildings and contents insurance might be invalid. Ensure you're covered for accidents – those no-win/no-fee liability claims can be astronomical. Suggest that your lodger get contents cover for their own stuff; your policy will probably not include it.
- **Check with your leaseholder.** They might forbid subletting.
- **Vet your lodger.** For your own safety, do the same thorough reference checks you'd do for a tenant (see Chapter 8 'How to find a good tenant').

- **Tick the safety boxes.** You have the same responsibilities as a normal landlord, described in Chapter 7 'Tick the legal boxes'.

To avoid adding to the red tape, don't take more than two lodgers – that will push you into HMO territory. Also, share a bathroom or kitchen with your lodger and keep access to their bedroom for cleaning, otherwise it's much harder to give notice.

The following will make your life, and theirs, easier:

- Ask for a month's rent in advance and a deposit – usually another month's rent. You don't have to protect the deposit in an official scheme
- Get your lodger to set up a standing order for the rent, so you won't have to nag them every month
- Have a house guide. Apart from useful information on the appliances and area, include a set of house rules you'd expect them to observe, for example on smoking, pets, visitors, cleaning and so on.

Now that we've covered the tried and tested principles for all tenant relationships, even short ones, we'll zoom in on the dos and don'ts for specific groups – including friends who share, friends with benefits and man's best friend.

CHAPTER 10

The dos and don’ts for six tenant types

In this chapter:

- **Why lets with pets are a good idea – and how to make them work**
- **Trade tips to get it right with young families, sharers and students**

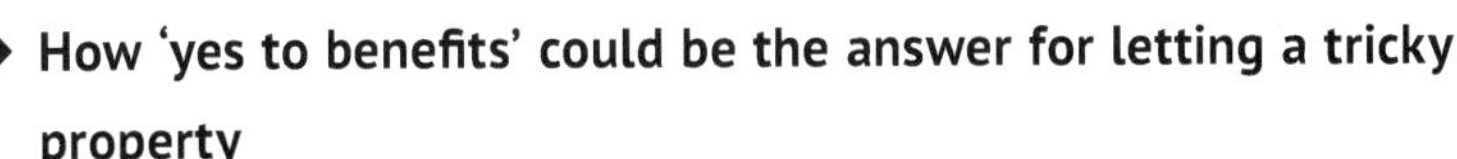

- **How ‘yes to benefits’ could be the answer for letting a tricky property**

- **What you must, can and don’t have to do for disabled tenants.**

News flash: renting is no longer only for the young. More than half of tenants are now over 30 and a third of them have children, according to the English Housing Survey. Thanks to Britain’s housing crisis, older renters and families are the fastest growing tenant types. In fact, rental homes around top schools nowadays demand a premium on a par with that in the sales market. Once it was a given that little Oliver and Amelia’s parents owned their home; now they might well be renting it.

Diversity is on the rise at every level of the lettings market. In London, a new breed of lifestyle renters with mid to high incomes choose to rent, even though they could buy, as they want to be free and mobile without worry about upkeep. These renters will pay as much as 80% more than an area’s going rate for a swanky new build let, the property giant CBRE has found. At the same time, government data shows almost a fifth of working private renters get housing benefit – a figure that has more than doubled in the six years since the financial crisis.

This all brings new intricacies to letting. Even if you never meet your tenants, providing their temporary home requires you to have some idea of how they live. Only then can you manage well. In this section, we'll arm you with all you need to know about every tenant profile – even the four-legged variety.

What you can't discriminate on

Under the Equality Act 2010, you cannot discriminate on age, gender, race, religion, sexual orientation or disability. Beyond that it's your choice to whom you let your home.

Pets

Here's another stat for your collection: almost half the households in Britain own a pet, says the Pet Food Manufacturers' Association. As tenants grow older and more established, more of them have pets. By allowing Fee-Fee and Frodo, you can widen your pool and attract better, longer-term tenants. Target the army of labradoodle lovers with adverts that state 'pets considered'.

You're not legally obliged to accept pets, though, and animal charities advise against putting them into flats without gardens. Plus, your flat's lease will often ban pets – so check that first.

What about chewed carpets and scratched sofas? Manage the risk by following the 'Lets With Pets' guide from the Dogs Trust (letswithpets.org.uk):

- **Check pet references.** Require a reference from a previous landlord or vet. It should say whether the pet is well-behaved and its owner responsible. A landlord should also state how long said pet lived in the house and if it caused damage or nuisance.
- **Ask for a bigger deposit.** By law, you have to protect the full amount in a government-backed scheme.

- **Add pet clauses.** The tenancy contract should permit the named pet and no others, and require the tenant to pay for any damage caused by their pet. They must also commit to a thorough professional carpet and upholstery clean at the tenancy's end. Lastly, you could retain £300 from the deposit two months after the tenancy ends in case there are fleas. Get the clause wording from 'Lets With Pets'.
- **Consider a pet policy.** You can download a sample policy with more detail on pet expectations from 'Lets With Pets'.

Very few landlord insurance policies cover accidental pet damage. Make it clear that this won't count as wear and tear, but that your tenant will have to pay for it. If you still want insurance cover on top of that, you'll have to hunt around for a specialist policy.

You might be worried about pets living in your home, but most of the risks can be reduced. Don't just say no. Being open-minded can bag you a great – and grateful – tenant.

Atishoo! Hidden cat hairs come back to bite owner

Your own pets can cause problems for tenants long after you've left your home. More than a year after Carol started letting out her two-bedroom Surbiton flat, her second tenant – who was allergic to cat hairs – struggled to breathe and broke out in welts as soon as he moved in. This was after the first set of tenants, who didn't have a pet, had professionally cleaned the carpets. That, it turned out, wasn't enough: hairs from Carol's cat had remained stuck to the underside of the sofa. She paid for another round of professional cleaning, this time for the carpets, upholstery andmattress. Finally the welts were gone.

Young families

A million families with children joined the private rental sector in the past decade, the English Housing Survey shows. Spare a thought for those worst hit by the housing crisis: the tweens who have had to move homes, schools and friends again and again because Mum and Dad can't afford the rent. As house prices soar and supply fails to keep up, rental demand from families will grow.

Despite visions of Junior decorating the walls with three-headed stickmen, letting to families is often a wise move for landlords. Because they'd like to keep their children in the same school, families make for stable, responsible tenants.

Here's how to make family lettings work for you:

- **Unfurnished please.** Families tend to have their own furniture. If your property is a house in the catchment area of a good school, attract families by offering to let it unfurnished.
- **Ensure it's long haul.** Avoid letting to families who want a stop-gap home. A second-floor flat with stairs but no lift won't work for anyone with a buggy. Likewise, a small second bedroom won't suit a one-child family for long if they're expecting a sibling. Ask about their current home: be wary if they are moving from somewhere bigger, or if they don't know the area at all. Be especially wary if the property is clearly not suited but is in the catchment area of a good school – they might be renting short term just to get their children in, then move elsewhere, leaving you with a potential void.
- **Make it safe.** If you do let furnished, remove anything that can be dangerous to young kids, such as glass tables, or at least let the tenants store it elsewhere. Fasten bookcases to the wall. And allow tenants to fit stair gates and safety locks to cupboards, as long as they make good when they leave.
- **Consider longer tenancies.** Offering a two- or three-year tenancy will give a family the school stability they need and protect you against void periods. You can build rent rises

into the contract. However, bear in mind that you could then not easily end the tenancy before the term is up if, say, you want to sell or they breach the contract.

Sharers

In many cities there is demand from groups of friends – usually professionals aged 25 to 40 – who want to share a home to save costs. This can be a lucrative market for you, especially if you charge rent individually per room. You also spread your risk as the tenants are all earning rather than relying on one breadwinner.

Some properties simply suit sharers, not families, for example a three-bedroom flat with no outside space. To target professional sharers, your house must be in a desirable area and kitted out with the furniture they'd expect. It should be near transport links and, if not in London, have at least two parking spaces.

To let to sharers successfully, you need to consider:

- **Will local rules allow it?** In some areas you'll need an additional licence and possibly planning consent for a house in multiple occupation (HMO) if letting to three or more unrelated people (see Chapter 7 'Tick the legal boxes'). However, some councils, for example in parts of Oxford, won't grant any more of these. Check with your council to find out if you need a licence.
- **Maximise stability.** Lets to sharers tend to be less stable than to families. Find out how strong your prospective tenants' bond is before you let: rows are less likely between friends than between souls who randomly found each other on Gumtree.com. Bear in mind, though, that you might still end up with more people in your property than you bargained for. If any of the tenants start a relationship, their newfound love could move in, too – and that's very hard to police, as you can't ban guests.
- **More work, more costs.** Letting by room means you have to collect the rent individually, with all bills included – landing you with yet more paperwork and costs. Turnover is higher

than for a couple or family: every time someone leaves, there are marketing charges, referencing fees and potential voids.

- **Is the rent really more?** All the above will eat into your returns. And if there's a shortage of family homes in your area, you might not make any more from sharers than from families in the first place.
- **Be honest with yourself.** There's an emotional question, too. If your property has been your family home, filled with memories of your children's mud pies and grazed knees, you might want to let to a family rather than sharers.

Students

Though scenes from the student sitcom *Fresh Meat* live long in the memory ('You can *study* drugs? Now they tell me'), these lettings are not all bathtubs filled with beer. A student house is where a bunch of 20-year-olds living away from home for the first time will forge love affairs, life-long friendships, careers and, yes, hangovers.

Now that students are no longer paid to be at uni, instead racking up debts close to the earnings of a mediocre MP, they expect more than damp hovels crammed with lumpy beds and flimsy flat pack. They prefer houses with gardens in vibrant student areas near the campus, shops and clubs – they don't own cars and don't want to walk far. A three-bedroom terrace, where you can often turn one reception room into a fourth bedroom, is usually ideal, as students are budget conscious.

There's money to be made, though. Students are exempt from council tax so can pay more rent. If you let by room, you'll make even more. They're predictable, too. You know exactly when they'll leave, by which time you can have signed up the next year's tenants with virtually no voids (though in some university towns you might have a gap over the summer holiday – check with local agents).

Here's how to get it right:

- **Start with the big questions.** What sort of owner are you, and what sort of tenant do you want? If you have a strong tie to your home and you want it to be looked after just as you would, then don't let to students.

- **Check HMO rules.** As with sharers, you might need an additional licence and perhaps planning permission for an HMO (read more in Chapter 7 'Tick the legal boxes'). Also, your council might not allow any new HMOs in your area – in which case, forget about a student let.
- **Furnish fully (and durably).** At the top of the market, international students prefer hotel-style studios with flat-screen TVs, stone worktops and access to private gyms. You don't have to go that far: apart from the usual supplies to a furnished property (see Chapter 6 'Prep and promote your property'), a double bed, generous desk and lockable door in each bedroom is all most students want. Also provide a shared TV in the living room and ample storage in the kitchen (a cupboard, fridge shelf and freezer drawer per person), but no kettle, toaster, plates or pans as they'll have their own. Furniture should be durable – no silly sofa legs, please – but basic, or students will think they're paying too much. Bike storage is a bonus.
- **Do extra checks.** Most students don't have references, simply because they are too young to have built up a history. Ask for a recommendation by their college, since they could lose their place if they misbehave. Also get a guarantor, usually their parent.
- **Educate upfront.** The wee darlings won't have learnt to change light bulbs or clean out the washing machine soap drawer. Enlighten them to such household joys, possibly with a session at the start of the tenancy or at least with a detailed house guide.
- **Hedge against high repair costs.** Draw up a detailed inventory and do inspections. Without that you'll get nowhere – deposit protection schemes are usually sympathetic to students. Make it clear that they have to leave the house as

they found it, or pay for repairs. Nevertheless, brace yourself for more wear and tear than with a family.

- **Involve parents.** Speak to their guarantors if cleanliness or damage needs addressing. (Swift had one set of male student tenants who failed to clean for what looked like an entire year.) Don't leave this until the end of the tenancy.
- **Avoid tenant turnover.** Include a clause in your contract stating that if one tenant leaves, the others have to find a replacement or pay the full rent.
- **Pay the bills.** Students expect all bills to be included, so factor that into your returns.

- **Set renewal deadlines.** Give them plenty of time to decide on renewing the tenancy and tell them by which date you need an answer. Otherwise they might give notice at the eleventh hour, leaving you in the lurch.
- **Don't forget your mortgage.** Not all lenders agree to student lets; check with yours.

Like any other tenant, students have a right to 'peaceably enjoy' their home – and for four or five students living together, that will include parties. But that's often not the main cause of problems with student lets; rather, it's when they're clueless and inconsiderate yoofs. Keep a light touch, but apply a firm hand when needed and you'll get your house back *sans* ciggy burns on the walls.

Tenants on benefits

Few landlords want to let to people on benefits – just count the number of online ads saying 'no children, no dogs, no DSS', as if they're worse than animals. (DSS refers to the now-defunct Department of Social Security, which used to run welfare payments.) Say the words 'housing benefit' and *Shameless*'s lager-swilling, work-shy Frank Gallagher might spring to mind. 'I promise I'll always be there for you,' he says to one of his 11 children in the Channel 4 drama, 'as long as I'm collecting your benefits.'

But that's not true anymore, if it ever was. Middle-income earners made up two-thirds of all new housing benefit claimants in the past six years, reports the National Housing Federation. The 18% of private tenants who work but now also get housing benefit can be a good fit for a cheaper property, especially one that's far from transport links or near an eyesore that would make it harder to rent on the open market. It may even yield a tidy profit.

Why? Because of the way in which the government decides how much housing benefit someone can claim. At the time of writing, housing benefit is slowly becoming part of the new universal credit, along with five other benefits. But the way in which the housing slice is calculated will be more or less the same.

Here's the low-down. Britain is carved up into rental market areas, each with a set amount of Local Housing Allowance (LHA) that will be paid to a person or family depending on how many bedrooms their situation entitles them to. It's usually set at the 30th percentile for the whole region, meaning it's based on the cheaper rents.

In Leeds, for instance, the state will pay £530 a month for a family of four to rent a two-bedroom home, whether it's an ex-council shoebox or a mansion with a glass car lift, a cigar room and a mini shark tank for the kids – as long as it has only two bedrooms. (The tenant has to make up the shortfall if they really want that shark tank. And the number of bedrooms is tied to the tenant's circumstances: a single person under 35 will only get enough for a room in a shared house, not a three-bedroom flat. Singles over 35 get to upgrade to a one-bedder of their own.)

That means you can price your flat at the exact level of LHA in your area (tinyurl.com/lha-search), which you know the government will pay. Advertise that you'll accept DSS, then sit back as tenants on benefits queue round the block for the chance to live in your well-maintained property – allowing you to cherry pick the best ones. They'll likely stay on, too, as it's so hard for them to find decent private rented homes. (We are not advocating ripping off taxpayers as you rent out a hovel to the hard-up who have nowhere else to go. By law, you must still be a responsible landlord who provides a safe home.)

Nevertheless, many lettings agents have blanket policies to accept no housing benefit. Where's the catch, then? Ahem...universal credit is paid directly to the tenant to help them take responsibility. Of course, the odd one might spend it on a flat-screen TV rather than the rent (though you can apply to be paid directly if the tenant is two months in arrears. Processing is slow, so don't wait until it hits the fan – tell the housing benefit officer early on).

Payments are also made in arrears, not upfront like your rent. Applications can take ages, leaving you out of pocket in the meantime. Tenants who haven't paid the deposit or rent with their own cash have less to lose – so could be less likely to look after your home. And, perhaps most fundamentally, when housing benefit tenants are given notice, councils routinely tell them they must stay put until the bailiffs arrive to qualify for any help in being rehoused. (This is incorrect advice, which you can take action against – we tell you how in Chapter 13 'When things go wrong'.)

If you're prepared for the extra work, though, these lets can be socially and financially satisfying:

- **Hedge your bet.** Ask for a bigger deposit and/or a guarantor with a job and a home they own.
- **Get clued up.** Amid the changing housing benefit system, many council officials are clueless or struggle to deal with poorly trained central government staff. Mistakes are common; guidance on universal credit is still sparse. In the meantime, get familiar with the mind-numbing *Local Housing Allowance Guidance Manual*.
- **Stay in the loop.** Get your tenant to sign a letter of authority allowing the housing benefit staff to talk to you about the progress of their application. Be nice to said staff and keep them on your side. Also get your tenant's national insurance number – the reference number used for universal credit claims.

- **Talk to your tenant.** Ask all new tenants if they get universal credit. If they do, find out on which date in the month they get their payment, so you can collect the rent.
- **Keep your eyes open.** Any existing tenant can apply for housing benefit once they are in your property – and you won't know unless they tell you. Look out for the signs: they might ask for a rent statement or a letter confirming a tenancy, have lost their job or be in rent arrears.
- **Get consent.** Check that your lender and insurer will allow these lets. Not all do.
- **Advertise to your audience.** Besides welcoming benefits in your property portal listing, also advertise on the specialist website dssmove.co.uk.

Friends with benefits prove a match made in lettings heaven

Ailsa only found out that her tenants had gone on to housing benefit when they asked her lettings agent for a tenancy confirmation letter. However, the young married couple turned out to be a dream let. Shop assistant Anna, 25, and gardener Peter, 29, did not earn enough to make ends meet after having their first child, so they needed housing benefit for the £1,100-a-month rent.

That's cheap for London, as Ailsa's 1930s maisonette was almost next to one of the busiest dual-carriageways into the capital. Yet Peter and Anna looked after the two-bedroom flat as if it were their own – even fixing bathroom taps and papering feature walls of their own accord (with Ailsa's permission).

Disabled tenants

About 5 million people have mobility problems, yet only 5% of homes in England are accessible to wheelchairs, reports the charity Leonard Cheshire Disability. Because of this hidden housing crisis, disabled people often stay longer when they do find a home that works.

What should you do if you'd like to target this market, or if your current tenant becomes ill or injured? Here are the dos, don'ts and don't-have-tos:

- **Clarify your tenant's needs.** Disabled needs vary a lot. Talk to your tenant so you can adapt the contract and house to suit them from the start.
- **Don't discriminate.** By law, you can't refuse to let to someone who is disabled, or evict them, just because you think the property won't work for them. (Shelter.org.uk lists all disabled tenants' rights.) However, you can say no if it's been your main home and you don't use a managing agent, or you still live there and would share a bathroom or kitchen with a lodger.
- **Change how you do things.** Legally you have to adapt any practices that disadvantage a tenant because of their disability. For example, you can't refuse a guide dog under a 'no pets' clause.
- **Provide reasonable extras.** You have to provide 'auxiliary aids' if the tenant asks. These must be reasonable requests (given the tenancy length, cost, disruption and so on) without which it would be hard or impossible for the tenant to make full use of the property. Examples are a tenancy agreement in CD format; supplying a portable ramp or removing a bulky piece of furniture; replacing taps or door handles that the tenant can't use; fitting a visual doorbell for a deaf person; painting doors dark to be seen more easily. You could get a grant for this – more on that shortly.

- **No physical changes required.** You have no obligation to alter how the property is built or designed. For instance, you don't have to turn the bathroom into a walk-in shower, build ramps, widen doors or fit a stair lift. (Phew. Doing all that would cost around £20,000.)
- **Permit reasonable requests.** Though you won't have to pay if your tenant asks to make physical changes themselves, you must not unreasonably refuse. (See citizensadvice.org.uk for the criteria.)
- **Get a grant.** It's possible to get funding, or small supplies such as portable ramps, from your local social services (gov.uk/disabled-facilities-grants). You or your tenant can apply for this. Otherwise you can come to a mutual agreement about the cost.
- **Advertise appropriately.** Once your property is accessible, you can market it on specialist sites, such as accessible-property.org.uk and thehouseshop.com.

You might have noticed a theme in this chapter: where there's more money on the table, there's also more work. Stick to the advice above, though, and the trade-off can be worth it in more ways than one – warming not only your pocket, but also your heart by meeting a real need.

Part 4
Paperwork

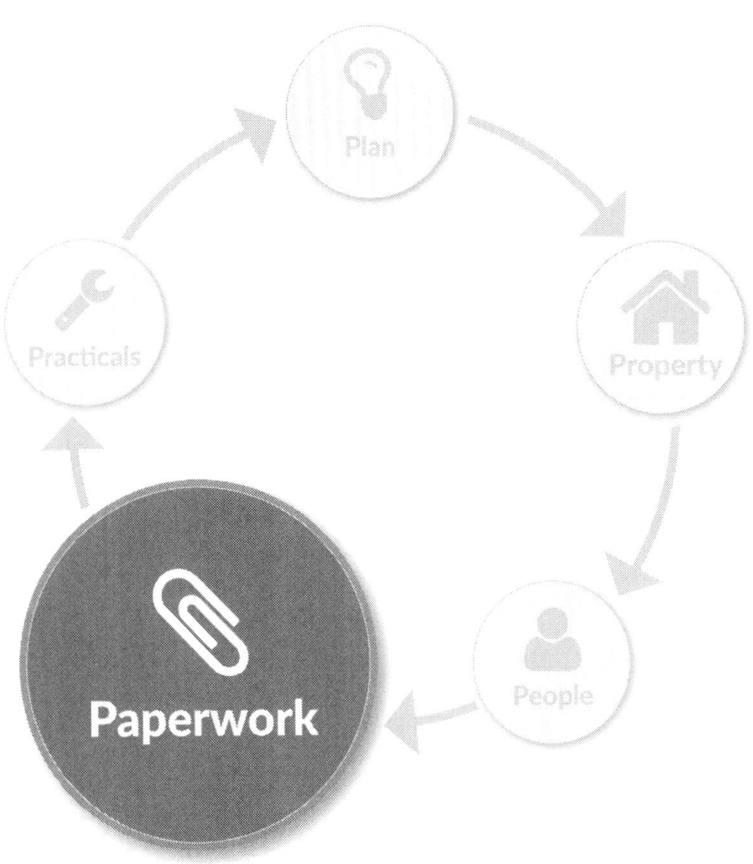

CHAPTER 11

Get the contract admin right

In this chapter:

- **Ten commandments for a bulletproof tenancy agreement**
- **Essentials made easy: deposit protection and three more legal musts**
- **The ins and outs of inventories, check-ins and house guides.**

What a difference one word makes. For 60 years after the First World War, private renting in Britain declined, dropping from almost 80% to little more than 10% of households. In a backlash against slum landlords like the 1950s landlord Peter Rachman – who led to the creation of the word 'Rachmanism' for tenant exploitation – successive laws have allowed a tenant to rent property at a low rate for as long as *two generations*. As landlords exited in droves, the lack of rental homes made it hard for people to move jobs, harming the economy.

Then Margaret Thatcher's regime said the magic word in an obscure housing act in 1988: 'Shorthold'. Under the new assured shorthold tenancies (ASTs), owners could suddenly let at market rates and always get their homes back after a short term. When buy-to-let mortgages came in on the strength of that in 1996, the industry took off. Today almost 20% of households rent privately – and Britain's housing shortage will likely see that grow even more.

In this section we'll go through the ABC of AST contracts, plus all the other paperwork you need at the start of a let: deposits, inventories, house guides, utility bills and the nitty gritty you've got to remember to avoid losing the right to end the tenancy easily.

Before we dive in, though, a quick legal primer on the lettings process. An offer is only guaranteed once both parties have signed the tenancy agreement. Offers fall through mainly because tenants fail their reference checks or they change their mind and pull out. This is very rare, though, once they've put down money. That's why it's a good idea to charge a holding deposit – we'd suggest £500 – to reserve the property. Confirm in writing that it's non-refundable if they back out.

A good process looks like this:

1. The tenant makes you an offer on the rent, tenancy length, move-in date and any furnishing requests
2. Both parties negotiate until all agree
3. You confirm the tenant's offer in writing, saying that it's 'subject to contract'. (That crucial little phrase means you won't inadvertently create a verbal or written contract without a formal tenancy agreement)
4. The tenant gives their reference information and pays a holding deposit
5. You check the references. If they're not spotless, you both agree any final changes – for example, a bigger deposit – or in extreme cases walk away from the deal. If you are the one pulling out, you should refund the holding deposit
6. Both parties sign the tenancy agreement
7. Your tenant pays the full deposit and first month's rent. Their holding deposit becomes part of this
8. Release keys for check-in only after their deposit has cleared.

Ten musts for your tenancy agreement

In almost all lets you'll have an AST by law. That gives you and your tenant certain rights and duties that you can't wriggle out of, even if you scribble 'this is not a tenancy' in big red letters all over your contract or you don't have a contract at all.

Any unfair clauses that break the law, like saying you can visit without warning, will be invalid. Likewise, any legal obligations that are left out in the contract will still apply, but it's best to have it all in writing for clarity (gov.uk/private-renting-tenancy-agreements).

So, what does the law say and what should you add to your contract? Here are the 10 most important points:

1. **Tenancy length.** By law, you can't end an AST before six months, so there is no point in having an initial fixed term that's any shorter than that. You can make it longer, but some lenders won't allow terms of more than a year. This is because you then cannot get rid of the tenants before the period is up, unless there is a serious breach like rent arrears. Tenancies beyond three years have to be executed as a deed. In practice, very few tenants would want to commit for that long; 12-month tenancies tend to strike the best balance between freedom and security.
2. **Rent.** State the rent and how it's paid (monthly, in advance and to a specific account). Say when the rent will be reviewed; we'd suggest annually. Unless your contract provides for a rent rise, you cannot increase it before the end of the fixed term.
3. **Basics.** Include all landlord and tenant names, the property's address and the start date. State if any part of the property is excluded, such as a garage. If there is more than one tenant, each person is 'jointly and severally liable' for the full rent. That means if one leaves or stops paying, the others still have to pay the full amount (not just their portion) for the rest of the term. Explain this to sharers – it's quite a commitment.
4. **Obligations.** The law lays out landlords' and tenants' duties. However, you can add clauses on minor repairs. From bitter experience, Swift's contract spells out that tenants have to pay for appliances blocked by 'hair clips, coins or collar stiffeners' (which has prompted one new tenant to ask, 'Hey, man, are there problems with the drains in this place?'). It allows picture hooks as long as tenants make good when they leave, but bans 'Blu-Tack, sticky tape or glue' on the walls.

5. **Notice period and break conditions.** State that both parties have to give two months' notice to end the tenancy at or after the end of the fixed term (or your tenant could be entitled to leave with less or no notice). For longer terms, say if the tenancy can be ended early and how this can be done. The courts will deem a break clause unfair if it only applies to the landlord.
6. **Termination reasons.** Say that you can end the tenancy if certain grounds listed in the Housing Act 1988 apply, including rent arrears, late payments, property damage and – crucially for accidental landlords – that you used to live in the property and need to return (see info below).
7. **Deposit.** Name the amount, how it will be protected and that no interest will be paid. Also say what can be deducted from the deposit: damage, costs if the tenant breaches the contract, unpaid rent and unpaid bills. Specify any admin fees, otherwise they could legally be deemed part of the deposit that has to be protected and refunded.
8. **Bills.** State who pays the utilities and council tax. It's normally the tenants, but you might do it for a student let or HMO.
9. **Pets.** If you've agreed to animals, add the pet clauses suggested in Chapter 10 'The dos and don'ts for six tenant types'.
10. **Guarantor.** If there is one, they confirm that they will pay if the tenant defaults or commits a breach that costs the landlord. By default, a guarantor will be jointly and severally liable for the full rent in a shared house.

Play the accidental landlord's get-out-of-jail card

If you've lived in the rental property before and you might need to do so again, tell the tenant about this before they move in. Do it by letter (there's no specific form for this) and also in the contract.

This will qualify as a 'Ground 1 Prior Notification Notice', giving you an automatic right to take back the house – though you can only invoke this with two months' notice at or after the end of the fixed term. In any subsequent eviction battle, a judge must side with you on this ground, as long as you warned the tenant about it from the start.

We could fill the rest of this book with boring clauses, but instead we'll point you to the government's free model AST contract (download it at tinyurl.com/ast-contract). If that doesn't suit you, you can buy contracts for a few pounds from the legal stationer Oyez (oyezstore.co.uk).

You can't use ASTs for lets shorter than six months, where the tenant is a company, the rent exceeds £100,000 a year, or for lodgers (see info below).

Winnie the Pooch gets her name in print

James's previous tenants had asked consent to have a dog, which then turned into two cats without his knowledge. So when his new tenants asked to keep a small, well-behaved dog, he agreed – provided they paid a bigger deposit and gave a pet reference from their former landlord. It was the picture they sent of the golden-haired Dandie Dinmot Terrier, ball in mouth, that had swayed James – 'I don't think they could have sent a cuter dog photo to get me to say yes!' – but this time there was no ambiguity in his contract: 'The Landlord grants permission for the Tenant(s) to keep a pet (one dog) named Winnie ("The Pet").' Children often don't get named in contracts, but this pooch did.

The paperwork for lodgers

You can more or less make your own rules for lodgers. To rent a room in your home, you grant a 'licence to occupy', not a full tenancy, so it's much easier to get rid of a lodger. That applies only while you live there – if you move out, your lodger could become a full tenant by default. Legally you don't need a contract, but it's wise to have one to prevent wrangles later. Make sure the following is in yours:

Access. Lodgers should not have exclusive use of any rooms. If they do, you'll need to go to court to evict them. So say in your contract that you have shared use of the bathroom or kitchen, and that you have access to clean their bedroom.

Fixed term. State the length of tenancy. Your lodger can't give notice during this period, unless there is a break clause. However, you can still give them notice mid-term.

Notice period. The legal default is that your lodger must give notice of at least four weeks (if they pay weekly) or one month (if they pay monthly). Again, you have it easier. Unless your contract says otherwise, you only have to give 'reasonable notice' to quit. This means the length of the rental payment period – so if they pay rent weekly, that's just one week's notice.

Room use. Mention that the room is for the lodger to live in, not for running a business from, so you won't invalidate your insurance.

You and your lodger can end a tenancy at any time if you both agree. Your notice doesn't have to be in writing. You can then change the locks on your lodger's rooms, even if their belongings are still inside (though you have to return these). Also see Chapter 4 'Think ahead to save a fortune in tax' for the Rent-a-room tax scheme and Chapter 9 'How to keep a good tenant' for how to manage a lodger.

There's no such thing as a free deposit

Cash deposits used to be seen as free money – some landlords would just keep it anyway, even if there was no damage or unpaid rent. Therefore, since 2007, landlords are obliged to protect deposits in one of the three state-backed schemes within 30 days of receipt, or face having to pay tenants *up to three times* the deposit value. They'd also lose their right to end the tenancy easily. Still, the Centre of Economics Business Research found that around 300,000 landlords are thought to be breaking this law, failing to protect more than half a billion pounds in deposits.

The three official schemes are:

- Deposit Protection Service (DPS: depositprotection.com)
- My Deposits (mydeposits.co.uk)
- Tenancy Deposit Scheme (TDS: tds.gb.com).

All three offer both an insured service, where you keep the deposit but pay an insurance premium to cover this, and a free custodial service, lodging the funds directly with them. Daniel finds the DPS custodial scheme the easiest to use for landlords, as you can do everything online.

By law, you have to give your tenant and anyone who has paid part of their deposit (a parent, say) the following three documents within 30 days of receiving the deposit:

1. **Prescribed information.** This explains how the deposit is protected. *If you fail to issue this, it won't count that you've protected the deposit* – you can still be fined and be unable to end the tenancy without giving a reason. You can post, email or hand deliver this, but keep records so you can prove it was served.
2. **Certificate or receipt.** Hand the tenants a copy of the proof that the deposit has been protected.
3. **Scheme leaflet.** Each scheme requires that you send out its tenant pamphlet and, for the DPS, its terms and conditions.

Do you really need a deposit? Oh yes. Don't waive it out of desperation – not charging one lays you open to risk. A deposit also shows commitment and puts off chancers.

And how much should you charge? Six weeks' rent for unfurnished lets works well; you could do two months' rent for furnished. Asking more than two months' rent could give tenants a right to sub-let.

Lastly, make it clear to tenants that any advance rent payments and non-refundable admin fees are not part of the deposit, otherwise you might have to protect them too.

Other legal musts to remember

Besides sending tenants the prescribed information on how you've protected their deposit, you must also give them three more bits of paper before they move in. If you don't, you lose your automatic right to take your property back:

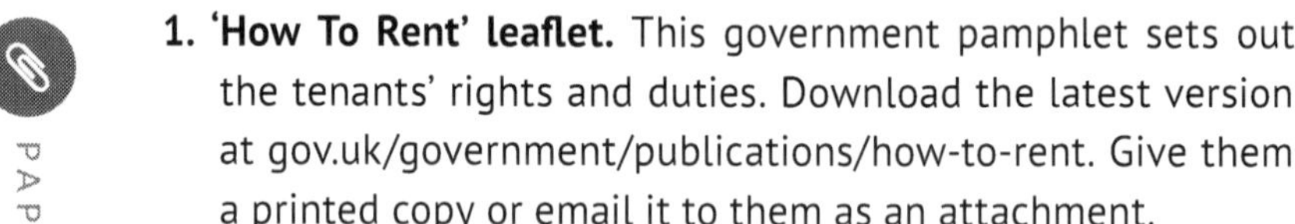

1. **'How To Rent' leaflet.** This government pamphlet sets out the tenants' rights and duties. Download the latest version at gov.uk/government/publications/how-to-rent. Give them a printed copy or email it to them as an attachment.
2. **Gas safety certificate.** If the property has gas, give new tenants a copy of the latest gas safety check, and again within 28 days after each annual test.
3. **Energy performance certificate.** You'll need an EPC before you advertise your rental (see Chapter 7 'Tick the legal boxes'). Give your new tenants a copy.

To prove you've done all this, ask tenants to confirm receipt for all three no later than when they sign the contract. They can do this by signing and dating a paper copy of each – that's the safest way – or by acknowledging receipt by email, if you've sent it electronically.

The ins and outs of inventories and check-ins

Do a professional clean

The inventory can only be done once your property is all sparklingly clean and completely ready, not while you're still clearing out cupboards. Give yourself at least a 48-hour margin for final preparations before your tenants check in – many a first-time landlord underestimates how long this takes.

Make sure all light bulbs are working and do a final garden tidy-up. And yes, you really do need a professional clean. That means 'hotel clean', not domestic clean. Carpets, too, need to be cleaned by a professional; DIY machines are not good enough – and by the time you've paid for the soap, they're not much cheaper anyway.

This will be a one-off expense for you, as you can then expect each set of tenants to pay for a professional clean at the end of their contract. Cleaning to the right standard will ensure the tenancy starts on a good footing. Done poorly, it often causes resentment, even after financial compensation.

Create a full inventory

Don't scrimp on the inventory. Get an independent clerk to create a full report on your property's contents and condition both before and after a tenancy. It will cost £100–£250, but the Deposit Protection Service says in any dispute it will have significantly more weight than one you did yourself.

Without an inventory, you can forget about claiming any damages. Besides protecting both you and your tenant, an inventory might also highlight any hidden maintenance issues.

A good inventory contains photos and detailed text descriptions. (In one case, an inventory stated: 'Bell, broken, to be rung with a spoon'.) Inventories used to be dictated and then typed, but there are now many apps to prepare them on a smartphone or tablet. Video inventories may sound like a good idea, but protection schemes dislike them because it's hard to find the relevant footage.

Make sure your clerk belongs to one of these professional bodies: the Association of Independent Inventory Clerks (AIIC: theaiic.co.uk) or the Association of Professional Inventory Providers (APIP: apip.org.uk).

When the tenant checks in, it's vital that they sign the inventory confirming it as a true record.

Check in the tenants

If you use an inventory clerk, they can also do the check-in for an extra charge (£80 for a two-bedroom flat). But it's straightforward to do this yourself.

A check-in includes:

- Hand over the keys
- Ask tenants to sign the inventory
- Give them your house guide (see info below)
- Point out the electricity fuse board, gas and electricity meters and where to turn off the mains gas in case of a leak
- Locate the stopcock for shutting off the water supply in an emergency
- Show them the boiler (if there is one) and the basics of how to use it
- Give an overview of how to use any key appliances
- Highlight any property quirks or maintenance issues that you are aware of
- Tell them whom to contact in an emergency such as a leak, or for repair requests.

In particular, newbie renters such as students won't know their responsibilities and need to be filled in on joys like cleaning dishwasher filters. Explain their duty to do such small jobs, to report more serious problems and to take prompt steps in an emergency. If they fail to do this, they might have to foot the bill for any damage they could have avoided.

There isn't time during a check-in to go through the entire inventory with a fine toothcomb. Though they should sign it on the day, give tenants a week to note any amendments.

What to include in your house guide

Don't hand over your very expensive, beautifully prepared home without instructions. Arming tenants with a written house guide could not only save you a fortune in avoidable damage to your property – and flats next door – but also spare you from silly calls on Christmas Eve. More info equals less bother.

Include the following:

Emergencies – where to switch off mains in case of a crisis with gas, water, electricity or drains. Give the phone numbers of whom to call: the National Gas Emergency Service, an emergency plumber and the water company, which also handles the mains drain.

Maintenance problems. Ask tenants to report signs of hidden problems: damp smells and flaking walls, overflowing pipes and short-circuiting fuses. Include phone numbers for you (or your agent) and your preferred tradesmen.

Ventilate. Tell them to air rooms, especially bathrooms, to stop condensation and black mould.

Blockages. Warn them not to put nappies, wipes, tampons, food or bones down toilets or drains.

Frozen pipes. When it's cold and the house will be empty for more than 12 hours, they should leave some heating on so the water system won't freeze.

Smoke alarms. Remind them to test smoke and carbon monoxide detectors regularly, and to replace the batteries.

Appliances. Include manuals for the washing machine, dishwasher and so on.

Useful info. Mention rubbish collection days, the nearest transport links, good restaurants and shops.

In a free extra to this book, you can download our house guide at accidentallandlord.info/extras.

Put utility bills in the right name

To avoid incorrect bills in your name (or that of a previous tenant), transfer utilities into the tenant's name where possible. You can do this for water and council tax, but tenants will need to set up their own gas and electricity accounts – they're free to choose any supplier in the deregulated energy industry.

It's easiest to transfer bills by email. Provide the property address, new tenant details and move-in date. Forwarding addresses for previous account holders help, but are not mandatory.

Lastly, set up a Royal Mail redirect for all your post. Letting your mail pile up alongside old minicab flyers in the communal hallway is a gift to identity fraudsters. Don't let them take you for a ride.

When tenants steal the whole house

Here's the worst that can happen to you as a landlord: your tenants steal your house. It's hit more than 20 London homeowners, including the veteran war reporter and historian Max Hastings, in cases investigated by the Met police at the time of writing. Sophisticated gangs target buy-to-let landlords who live far away and don't have mortgages. They gain access to the home by posing as tenants, then use the landlord's details to market and sell the property to some poor sod who thinks they're buying legitimately – only to have their half a million pounds or so disappear to Dubai as soon as it leaves their account. The landlord only finds out once said sod's lawyer comes knocking.

As Hastings put it: 'Why bother breaking in when you can steal the whole building?'

In a separate case in 2005, Brighton landlord Grahame Hawthorn's tenant took out a mortgage of more than £200,000 on the house and disappeared. The tenant had collected Hawthorn's post and used that to pose as Hawthorn.

Though these owners did eventually get their homes back, it involved nightmarish court cases and long wrangles to clear their names. Avoid an identity crisis – keep your details safe.

Hurrah, you've got your bulletproof (and bulldog-proof) contract signed, deposit protected and the four crucial bits of paper served. Your inventory is up to date, your tenants house-trained and your bills redirected. The flurry of paperwork at the start of your tenancy is finally over, but there's another one waiting for you at the end. You just can't get enough of this, can you?

CHAPTER 12

The nuts and bolts of ending a tenancy

In this chapter:

- **The nitty gritty of giving notice correctly, or letting the contract roll on**
- **How to check out your tenants without falling out**
- **What you can and can't deduct from the deposit (hint: you'll get less than you think).**

Warning: you can't just boot out your tenants – no matter whether you want to live in your house, sell it or they've been less than model and you want shot of them. The only way you can end a tenancy is by mutual agreement, or through a set legal process – if they don't play ball, you have to go to court.

The good news is that only 0.7% of private tenancies end up in court, Ministry of Justice figures show. In this section we look at the normal steps to end – or renew – a tenancy when all goes well. We also tell you how to handle check-outs and deposit deductions without getting into nasty disputes.

How to end (or extend) a tenancy fuss free

Should I renew or roll on?

If you reach the end of the fixed term and you want to let your tenants stay on, you have two choices:

- **Renew the tenancy.** You can sign another contract with a new fixed term. This means you can be sure of the rent for the whole new period, but you're also locked in – so you can't get your house back early to sell or move in. In other words, you're starting over.

- **Go periodic.** Alternatively you can let the tenancy roll on from week to week or month to month, depending on how you've charged rent so far. All the terms of the initial contract apply, except that you or your tenant can now give notice any time. Such a periodic tenancy gives you flexibility, but not much certainty. To go periodic, simply get your tenant to confirm in writing that they want to stay on.

Whether you renew or roll on, the end of the fixed term is the best time to raise the rent. See how in Chapter 9 'How to keep a good tenant'.

How to draft and deliver a notice

What if you want your house back? It's crucial to dot all the 'I's and cross all the 'T's when you give notice. If you draft one small detail wrong, or deliver it in the wrong way, the courts will throw it out – losing you months if there's an eviction battle down the line. So if there's even the slightest hint that a tenant might feed your notice to their unauthorised pet and stay put, take extra care. Most tenants, though, will comply with your request.

Brace yourself, then, for a dose of landlord legalese. We'll try and make this as painless as possible.

When can I give notice? At the end of the fixed term, you have an automatic right to take your property back, but *you still have to issue your tenants with a Section 21 notice.* This is a way of saying that the tenant hasn't done anything wrong, but you want your house back anyway.

Once the tenancy has gone periodic, you can serve a Section 21 any time.

When can't I give notice? A Section 21 won't be valid before the fixed term ends. To end the tenancy early, there are three other routes:

- You and your tenant both agree. This is called 'surrender' – more on that shortly
- A break clause in your contract allows it, and you follow it to the letter
- Your tenant commits a serious breach and you serve a Section 8 notice. This requires you to pick one or more reasons from a pre-written list, which we discuss in the next chapter.

At or after the term's end, you still can't serve a Section 21 if any of these are true:

- You've failed to give your tenants an energy performance certificate, gas safety certificate or 'How To Rent' leaflet (see previous chapter)
- You've failed to protect their deposit or give them the prescribed information on where their money is kept safe
- The property needs an HMO licence but doesn't have one
- The tenant has written to you to ask for repairs and the council has slapped you with an improvement notice to fix them – all *before* you issued the Section 21. (This new law prevents revenge evictions.)

Up yours! Tenant clobbers landlord over deposit papers

Landlord Swindells wanted their property back because tenant Ayannuga was in rent arrears. When the notice arrived, Ayannuga counter-sued for the full £950 deposit plus a £2,850 fine. You see, the landlord had protected the deposit and told the tenant about this in the contract and in a letter, but – horror of horrors – didn't send the prescribed information in the form of the deposit scheme's publicly available leaflet. And you know what? On appeal in 2012, the tenant won.

How much notice should I give? You must serve a Section 21 notice *at least two months* before the date you want your tenants to leave, which doesn't have to fall on the day they pay rent.

You can't serve any earlier than four months into the tenancy. In practice that means you can't force a tenant to move out on the exact last day of a six-month term – it will be a few days later at best.

Do I need to use a special Section 21 form? For tenancies that first started after 1 October 2015, you must use the government's Form 6A ('No Fault Possession Notice On An Assured Shorthold Tenancy', gov.uk/guidance/assured-tenancy-forms). Now try and say that form's name quickly.

How should I deliver it? Don't use recorded delivery, because if the tenant is out or refuses to sign, your notice won't be served. Use normal post and get a proof of postage receipt; the notice period starts when it arrives, so factor in a few days extra. To play it safe, take an independent witness to video you as you hand deliver. Email the tenant a copy of the notice for good measure.

When the tenant wants to leave

If your tenant tells you they're leaving, ask them to confirm it in writing.

How much notice should they give? Their notice period depends on when they give it:

At the end of the fixed term. Strictly speaking, your tenant is allowed to up sticks on the last day of the fixed term without any notice. That's the only day they have this right: before then they are bound by the contract to pay rent for the full term, and from the very next day the tenancy becomes periodic, meaning they must give at least one month's notice. Two or three months before the end of the fixed term, protect yourself by asking your tenants to confirm in writing if they want to stay – then you can plan ahead.

Once the tenancy has gone periodic. Unless your contract says otherwise, the default notice period for your tenant is at least a full month (if rent is monthly) or 28 days (if rent is weekly) – counted from the day on which rent is paid. So if they pay monthly rent on 1 January and give notice to quit the same day, they can leave on 1 February. But if they give notice on 3 January, the earliest they can leave is 1 March. Confused? You won't be alone – welcome to eviction law!

What if my tenant surrenders early? The simplest way to end a tenancy during the fixed term is when you both agree: your tenant gives up the property early and you accept their surrender. (Dressing up as Captain Maitland, to whom Napoleon raised the proverbial white flag, is entirely optional.)

If you reject it, they remain liable to pay rent for the rest of the fixed term. In practice, though, you don't want an angry tenant who might rip your house apart. Rather accept a surrender but ask tenants to pay the marketing costs plus rent for any void before a re-let. This incentivises them to keep the place spick and span for viewings.

The tenant can surrender by signing a written declaration, or by implying it with their actions – for example, if they remove all their stuff and leave the keys in the door. Whichever they do, respond and accept their surrender in writing.

There, all done for now. That didn't hurt a bit – did it?

The key to check out without falling out

Tenant check-outs are a bit like leaving the house with a toddler (or at least, with our toddler): preparation makes a big difference to the number of tantrums thrown.

All too often dream tenancies end in a row over deposit money. Nine times in ten that's because tenants don't know what they have to do to get their deposit back. By giving them a fair chance to get things right, however, you can part on good terms.

You can do this though a pre-arranged visit around six weeks before they move out, during which you can check that everything works as it should. Point out anything that they'd be charged for unless they fix it.

Swift's system is to email tenants their check-in inventory plus a detailed list of how they should leave the property to avoid deductions. It reminds them of often-forgotten items to clean (see info below); to replace blown light bulbs and leave all keys; and to take all their belongings or face removal charges. It also explains how to close utility bills and reclaim their deposit.

As a free extra to this book, download a tenant checklist for moving out from accidentallandlord.info/extras. Send this to your tenants as soon as you have their notice; it will save you no end of deposit wrangles.

The move-out day can simply be a case of the tenants leaving all the keys inside the property and closing the door. No one else has to be there.

Get an independent clerk (theaiic.co.uk, apip.org.uk) to take meter readings and compare the property's contents and condition to the check-in inventory. If it's the same clerk you used in the beginning, so much the better. This will cut the chances of a dispute to almost nil, and without this level of evidence you won't get far in front of an adjudicator.

This check-out inspection can happen with or without the tenants present. Doing it without them there prevents conflict, provided you've given them enough time to prepare. If you've done all of the above, or checked that your agent has, you should never have any arguments about deposit returns.

Allow a few days between the old tenants leaving and the new ones moving in, in case you need to fix anything or top up cleaning.

How clean is 'clean'?

The most disputed item in any deposit deduction is, without a doubt, cleaning. Standards differ, even among companies – so a receipt from a professional cleaning company doesn't prove that a property has been cleaned to the right standard. Tenants can feel offended when they've paid for this, or spent hours in marigolds themselves, only to be told there will still be a cleaning deduction.

One such set of departing tenants was livid when Swift said their cleaning wasn't good enough. Yet the new tenants, who insisted on moving in the next day, were just as livid about the same cleaning – precisely because it wasn't good enough.

This is a tough job to get right – once you find a good cleaner, hang on tight. Here's a non-exhaustive list of what a good professional clean should include:

- Washing machine soap drawer and door seal thoroughly cleaned
- Light fittings and all high-level surfaces, including the tops of doors and dado-rails, dusted
- Oven sparkling inside
- Fridge seals, inside and outside surfaces cleaned
- Kitchen cupboard doors and tops of cupboards wiped
- Extractor hood filter replaced (if applicable)
- Carpets professionally steam cleaned, not just vacuumed.

What you can and can't take off the deposit

By law, the deposit remains the tenant's property and you must return it to them within 10 days of you both agreeing how much they'll get back. Any amount in dispute will stay in state-backed protection until you sort out the issue.

There's no need to hold on to some deposit money for outstanding utility bills. Once you've taken final meter readings and a forwarding address in good faith, providers can't come after you.

You can deduct money for missing or damaged items, but you have to stick to strict rules. The main principle is that fair wear and tear always applies. You can't have new for old, for example, by demanding the full cost of a new replacement for something that wasn't new when the tenant moved in. You'd end up better off than you would have been at the tenancy's end with wear and tear taken into account. Such 'betterment' is banned.

To work out how much you can deduct, consider the item's quality and condition at the tenancy's start and its usual lifespan. The longer the let, the greater the wear and tear that is allowed. Even if the damage seems deliberate, you can't deduct any more than you could for the same accidental damage – repairs would cost the same.

Pick the most appropriate of three solutions:

- **Compensation.** If an item is damaged but still usable, you can deduct to make up for the loss in value or shorter lifespan
- **Repair.** If it can be cleaned or fixed, you can deduct that cost
- **Replacement.** If something is missing or damaged beyond repair, its replacement cost is its second-hand value at the end of the tenancy.

For example, a carpet stain would be seen in the context of how much of the carpet it affects; if it can be cleaned rather than replaced; whether it's so noticeable that it would affect the rent; how old the carpet is; and so on. In practice, this means the deductions you can make are usually a lot lower than you might have thought.

Thankfully, malicious damage is rare. Swift, for one, has never had a case of a tenant wrecking a place. What you will get, though, are things like scuffed walls, dead plants and blocked drains.

Be prepared for reasonable wear and tear. It's like seeing an old friend and being surprised at how much they've aged – the gentle decline that goes unnoticed when you live in your home can come as a shock when you return after several years. For high-traffic areas such as hallways, stairs, kitchens and bathrooms, expect to repaint as often as every three years, advises the Tenancy Deposit Scheme. Budget carpets might not last five years, but top-quality ones might keep going for two decades.

Only 0.6% of deposits are disputed, says the My Deposits protection scheme. In these cases, your scheme provides adjudication – usually by an independent solicitor. Their decision cannot be appealed, so make sure you submit all the evidence before the deadline given.

When tenants leave stuff behind

What do an elephant's foot, a box containing nail clippings and a crash test dummy have in common? They've all been left behind by tenants, reports the Deposit Protection Service. Among the other gems from their poll of more 1,000 landlords were a pair of synthetic breasts, a bowl with 17 live spiders and – inevitably – sex toys.

Funny as they may be, forgotten tenant belongings can cost you if you don't deal with them correctly. Tort law means your tenant is perfectly entitled to sue you two years down the line (with legal aid, mind) for dumping their synthetic breasts, unless you do the following.

Send a letter by recorded delivery to the tenant. If you don't have their new address, post it to your rental home in case they've set up mail forwarding. Say what items they've left and give a reasonable date when you'll dispose of them. (The law doesn't define a reasonable date.) Also include your contact details. Store the goods for the time mentioned. If you then sell them, the profit belongs to the tenant but you can deduct your costs.

Armed with this book, you have every chance of a tenancy among the 99.3% that don't go to court. In those 99.3% of cases, ending a tenancy is simply a matter of giving notice, preparing for check-out and returning your tenant's deposit – and you now know how to do all this without a hitch. But if you do have to deal with a problem tenant, we're here to help. In the next chapter it's time for some troubleshooting – including disappearances, damage and defaults.

CHAPTER 13

When things go wrong

In this chapter:

- **What to do if your tenant gets a dog, disappears or you don't get on**
- **Common-sense advice if they stop paying rent or cause damage**
- **If it comes to it, three clear-cut steps to get evictions right.**

As councils grapple with Britain's housing crisis, they routinely advise tenants on lower incomes to stay put after their landlords have asked them to leave. Officials tell these tenants, who struggle to find affordable homes to rent, that they can't get state help until they're made homeless when the bailiffs arrive. That can force their landlords to spend around four months and £400 on an eviction through the court. (If the landlord represents themselves, that is; with a solicitor it rises to £1,500 or more.)

'How can the council do this? Totally shocked!'

Our family has just returned from living abroad and are planning on moving back into our property that we have been letting out. We got a call from the letting agents saying that our tenants have advised them that they cannot find another property in their price range and the council is telling them to stay put. What?

> *It is not like we are property investors and are just trying to get higher rent. We do not have any other accommodation. My children need to have a roof overhead and be placed in school. How can the council do this? What action can we take and how long should we expect to be displaced? Totally shocked!*
>
> Posted by Aimlessly on Mumsnet

This doesn't mean the tenants are chancers. A decorator friend of ours, who has three young children and a wife who works as a night cleaner, was told the same thing by his council when their landlord gave notice and they failed to find somewhere else in their budget to rent.

'That's not right,' he told us. 'I'm a good man and I don't want to do that to my landlord, but what else can we do?' He persevered and eventually found a new home without putting his landlord through an ordeal.

We think this practice by councils is an unethical cop-out that amounts to stealing from landlords. It's unfair to incoming tenants, too, who cannot move in. The housing minister has since written to all local councils, telling them not to advise tenants to wait for the bailiffs but to help them once the landlord has given notice. If you're in this boat, rub that under your council's nose.

In this chapter we tell you what to do in this and other what-if scenarios, before taking you through the legal process for evictions.

What if...

Rest assured, these situations are rare, and even then an eviction is the last resort. Here's what to do if:

The tenant sublets, runs a business or gets a pet

These are all breaches of the tenancy agreement that you might pick up during an inspection, even if the tenant tries to hide it by, say, locking the dog in the car. You or your agent should talk to the tenant. Also remind them in writing of the breach and ask them to put it right. Follow up to check that they have done so. That said, these are unlikely to be grounds for eviction if you take it to court: that would be up to the discretion of the judge.

With unauthorised pets, it might be worth accepting them in your property, as long as it's not a flat with a head lease that bans animals (and said animals aren't five Rottweilers whose owner works full time). As private renting grows, more families with pets apply to be tenants. Amend your contract with clauses on a bigger deposit, cleaning and damage costs, as explained in Chapter 10 'The dos and don'ts for six tenant types'.

In some cases, you might want to look the other way. It can be hard to prove subletting: if extra people who are not listed on the contract are living at the property, they could claim they are only visiting for a few weeks – and you can't refuse that. Likewise, it's difficult to stop a tenant running a business from home. If they still pay rent on time and look after the house, consider keeping schtum.

But if there's damage or neighbours complain – like when one tenant's teenage nephew forever smoked with his mates while Justin Bieber boomed away, or when a photographer set up a studio in a basement flat without the landlord's consent, drawing a stream of clients who'd buzz upstairs by mistake – you'll need to have that chat.

You don't get on with your tenant

Unless the tenant has broken the contract, or you can mutually agree an early termination, it's too bad. You'll have to wait until the end of the fixed term to give them notice. Manage the relationship as best you can by following the tips on communication in Chapter 9 'How to keep a good tenant'.

The tenant disappears

Vanishing acts don't always mean the tenant has done a runner. They might be in hospital, on a round-the-world trip, burying their dad or – eek – in jail. Resist the temptation to chuck out their stuff, change the locks and re-let, as that's illegal. You still have to serve notice and, if necessary, go to court to get your house back (as outlined below), unless you can prove implied surrender.

So don your finest deerstalker hat for a bit of detective work. Talk to the tenant's employer (you have their details from referencing), guarantor, neighbours and utility companies to find out when they left and where they went. Keep records for evidence.

Put a note through the door to say you'll visit your property in 24 hours. When you do, look for signs of abandonment: if they've taken all their belongings and left the keys, that's as close to implied surrender as you'll get. A pile of mail on the doormat, empty wardrobes and bare fridge are other giveaways. Take pictures and compare the contents to the inventory.

If you're absolutely sure they've gone, write to tell your council's tenant relations officer about this, and that you intend to change the locks and re-let. Store the tenant's stuff before taking back your property.

But if any of their belongings are still there and they haven't left keys, you have to follow a set legal process. Under new laws, you can only take back the property without a court order if the tenant owes at least two consecutive months' rent and you have given three warning notices – not only to the tenant, but also to other deposit payers and occupiers. You must give them at least eight weeks to respond. Remember to tell your rent guarantee insurer as soon as possible so you can claim for lost rent.

The tenant stops paying rent

Even good tenants can stop paying rent if they lose their job or split up with their other half. If you sense genuine hardship, informal negotiation tends to work best. The tenant usually wants to find a way forward, and in the long run this will still cost you less than a lengthy eviction. Try:

- **Reduced rent.** If the tenant is cash strapped for a short time, you could temporarily lower the rent.

- **Quick exit.** You could agree to a rent payment plan or waive any money owed if they agree to move out swiftly.
- **Benefits.** The tenant can apply for housing benefit. Under the new universal credit system, both you and your tenant can ask for their housing money to be paid directly to you if the rent is two months in arrears. Get your tenant to sign a letter authorising officials to discuss their application with you.
- **Council re-housing.** As we've seen at the start of this chapter, councils often tell struggling tenants that they must stay put until they're evicted or they can't get social housing. If that's the case, meet your tenant half way: apply to the court for accelerated possession (more on that soon) while they carry on paying rent and you both keep talking to the council.

However, if they won't talk to you at all, you might be dealing with a shyster who plays the system. You can then issue a Section 8 notice for their breach and take them to court. If they owe more than two months' rent, the judge must find in your favour. (Though that is not as straightforward as it sounds – the tenant may fight it; see anecdote below.) But if their arrears are less than two months' worth, or they keep paying late, it's up to the judge whether or not to evict. If you are allowed to serve a Section 21 notice, that is usually safer.

Deposit error descends into £30,000 arrears hell

After putting down three months' rent upfront, Nadia and Kevin's tenant – a 'friend of a friend' who was a single mother with twin teenage daughters – never paid rent again (see Chapter 8 'How to find a good tenant' for how this story began). However, they couldn't serve a Section 21 notice because they had protected her deposit too late, so they issued a Section 8 notice instead.

When they finally got a five-minute court hearing – almost a year after she'd stopped paying rent – the tenant had legal aid and counterclaimed for disrepair, harassment, trespass, loss of quiet enjoyment and late protection of the deposit.

'Only the last one had any basis in truth,' says Nadia. She and Kevin had completely renovated the place just before the tenant had moved into their three-bedroom house in Leytonstone, east London, so a claim for disrepair 'didn't seem possible'. But the tenant had changed the locks and refused them access, including the annual gas safety check or to check any of the alleged disrepair. The case was adjourned for a proper hearing nine months later. So far, it's cost them almost £30,000 in lost rent and legal fees, and their solicitor estimates it will take at least another eight months to get the tenant out.

'Never, *ever* issue a Section 8,' Nadia says. 'Make sure your paperwork is spotless and you have complied with everything you need to issue a Section 21 if you ever have to. And keep records of any issues that come up during the tenancy, such as repairs and how you dealt with them.'

If you've failed to protect the deposit within 30 days, your best bet is to refund it to the tenant immediately (less any deductions, such as rent arrears, that the tenant agreed to in writing). Get a stamped bank slip for the transfer or pay cash with a witness present, so you can prove you've paid it. Of course that will hurt, but it will hurt less than having to pay the tenant the full deposit plus a fine of treble that amount if they successfully counterclaim in court.

The tenant damages the property

As ever, talk first. If it's a bunch of youngsters, they might simply need to be put on the right track – as explained under the student section in Chapter 10 'The dos and don'ts for six tenant types'. Also write to them (and their guarantor parents) to recap your conversation, asking them to make good or pay for repairs.

Eviction is not guaranteed if you take your tenant to court over property damage alone. A judge may just order the tenant to fix what's broken instead of giving you your house back. Worse, your tenant can file a defence or even counterclaim to 'clear their name' – possibly with legal aid – dragging out the whole palaver for many months and many thousands of pounds. Get legal advice before you sue.

Vicars miss smoke signals of cannabis farm

Two vicars who live in the same Chiswick street were astounded to hear that one of the few houses between them had been turned into a cannabis factory, tapping the street's mains power. Tasteful curtains had hidden it all – until the police raid. The bill to repair a gutted property punched full of plant ventilation holes can be £25,000, literally sending your rental profits up in smoke.

To avoid this, check the holy heck out of would-be tenants (short of blood types and dental records). If they offer six months' rent upfront, drive a Range Rover and ask too many questions about the power supply, your crook alarm should wail.

Do regular inspections and keep in touch with the neighbours. Tell-tale signs include a spike in electricity bills, duct-tape and condensation in blacked-out windows, lights through the night and bags full of plant material and fertiliser outside. Obviously don't confront them but call the police. Then you *still* have to follow the court procedure to oust them via a Section 8 notice, otherwise you might end up in court yourself – charged with an illegal eviction.

How to evict a tenant

Getting a tenant out can take two weeks to eight months if all goes well – much longer if it doesn't. This process has three steps, which we'll discuss in a moment:

1. Give your tenant notice
2. Apply to the court for possession
3. Send in the bailiff.

Surprise, surprise, there's a lot of form filling. Find the government guide – and all the right forms – at tinyurl.com/eviction-guide.

For excellent advice and plenty of sympathy along the way, join a landlord association (Residential Landlords Association, rla.org.uk; National Landlords Association, landlords.org.uk; £50–£80 a year). Or subscribe to landlordlaw.co.uk for an easy but thorough do-it-yourself eviction guide (from £20 a month).

You could also get a reputable landlord eviction firm to do each step for a flat fee, from around £120 for giving notice (legal-forlandlords.co.uk, landlordaction.co.uk).

Step 1: give notice

Don't delay giving notice; it means you'll lose less rent – and less sleep. Serving it quickly gives you options: you can always decide not to act on it, but your hands are tied if you haven't issued it yet.

There are two types of notice under the Housing Act 1988:

Section 21. This gives you an automatic right to take your property back at the end of the fixed term, as long as you have followed the law perfectly throughout the tenancy and in drawing up the notice. You don't have to give a reason or accuse the tenant of anything. (See the start of the previous chapter for the finer rules on this.)

Section 8. Use this when a tenant causes so much grief that you want to see the back of them, but you can't serve a Section 21 because the tenancy has far more than three months to go. You

have to choose at least one reason from a set list of grounds. (See info below for details.)

Where appropriate, you can serve both notices at the same time and decide later which one to act on. Once issued, a Section 21 is valid for six months and a Section 8 for a year. If you want to go to court, you have to do so before it expires, or you'll be back to square one.

How to draft a Section 8 notice

When can (and should) I give a Section 8 notice? You can do so any time during the fixed term, as long as:

- You only use grounds 2, 8, 10 to 15 or 17 listed in Schedule 2 of the Housing Act 1988. These include rent arrears, property damage and anti-social behaviour
- Your contract must say that you can end the tenancy on any of these grounds.

However, certain grounds are stronger than others. Some are mandatory, so the judge automatically has to give you your house back. *The only mandatory ground on which you can claim during the fixed term is rent arrears of more than two months* (Ground 8). Less serious rent arrears (10), late payments (11), damage (13 and 15), anti-social behaviour (14) and lying (17) are all discretionary, which means the court can rule against you.

If you have discretionary grounds only, get legal advice before you do anything. In such cases it's almost always better to sit out most of the tenancy's fixed term and serve a Section 21 notice, which guarantees that you'll get your property back. That's less confrontational and can save you a nasty fight, even if you're really kicking out the tenant because he lied, trashed the place and tormented the neighbours.

Once the tenancy has gone periodic after the term's end, your Section 8 notice can use any of the Act's 17 grounds. However, by this point you're allowed to serve a Section 21, which is usually faster and simpler.

One exception is if you've lost your right to issue a Section 21 because you forgot to protect your tenant's deposit or give them a legally required bit of paper at the start of the tenancy. For accidental landlords, there is a way around this: if you've previously lived in your rental home and want to move back in, you can automatically get the property back on this basis (Ground 1). However, before the tenancy's start you must have warned the tenant in writing that this could happen, and you must serve a Section 8 notice at least two months before your return. You can only do this once the fixed term has ended.

How much notice should I give? The notice period for a Section 8 varies from two weeks to two months, depending on the ground you use. For serious rent arrears (Ground 8), it's two weeks.

Do I need to use a special Section 8 form? Indeed. Get it at tinyurl.com/eviction-guide.

How should I deliver it? In the same way as a Section 21 – see the previous chapter.

Step 2: go to court

If your tenant doesn't leave by the date set in the notice, you will need to apply to the courts for a possession order.

Don't do this lightly. Once you get on this fast train, you might not be able to get off for a long time. Your tenant could counterclaim and that will carry on – even if you withdraw your part of the case, which would also make you liable for their legal costs. Plus, the courts are in meltdown, so a contested case takes many months. Ensure your paperwork is faultless and only claim if your tenant won't be able to defend successfully.

There are two court routes, depending on which kind of notice you served:

- **Accelerated possession.** Formula One it's not, but this means a judge decides on the papers alone, without a hearing (unless you've made a mistake or your tenant files a viable defence) – saving you time and money. You can only use this route if you served a Section 21 notice, have a written tenancy agreement and don't claim owed rent money at the same time.
- **Standard possession.** This means you attend a court hearing and give evidence before a judge. It's your only option if you've issued a Section 8 notice. You can get a money judgement at the same time. If you're only seeking possession and rent arrears, you can speed things up slightly by filling in the forms via the possession claim online service (PCOL: https://www.possessionclaim.gov.uk/pcol).

The court usually orders possession within 14 days, or 42 days if the tenant would suffer exceptional hardship.

Step 3: send in the bailiff

If your tenant still hasn't budged by the date set in the court order, apply to the court to send a bailiff to evict them. That means yet another form and three to five weeks' wait. When the bailiff goes in, you must be there with a locksmith to take possession and change the locks.

You'd be very unlucky for things to go this far. Of the 33,000 or so eviction cases brought by private landlords in a year, less than a third go all the way to the bailiff turning up, Ministry of Justice data shows. That's only 0.2% of the 4.3 million private tenancies in England.

Whatever you do, don't harass

However tempting, it's against the law to lock your tenant out, cut off the utility supply, remove their belongings, take off doors or windows, refuse visitors or persistently disturb them. Serious harassment can land you with a criminal conviction, a fine and a hefty compensation claim from your tenant. If relations are fraught, leave no room for false accusations: deal only in writing or take an independent witness.

Not every problem tenant warrants an eviction. Often it's better to deal with issues through good communication, to manage them with, say, a new pet clause in the contract or to look the other way.

However, if you have no choice but to evict, the most important step is to pause and analyse the situation at the start: carefully work out which notice and court procedure to use. Get this wrong, and you could lose your case.

Part 5
Practicals

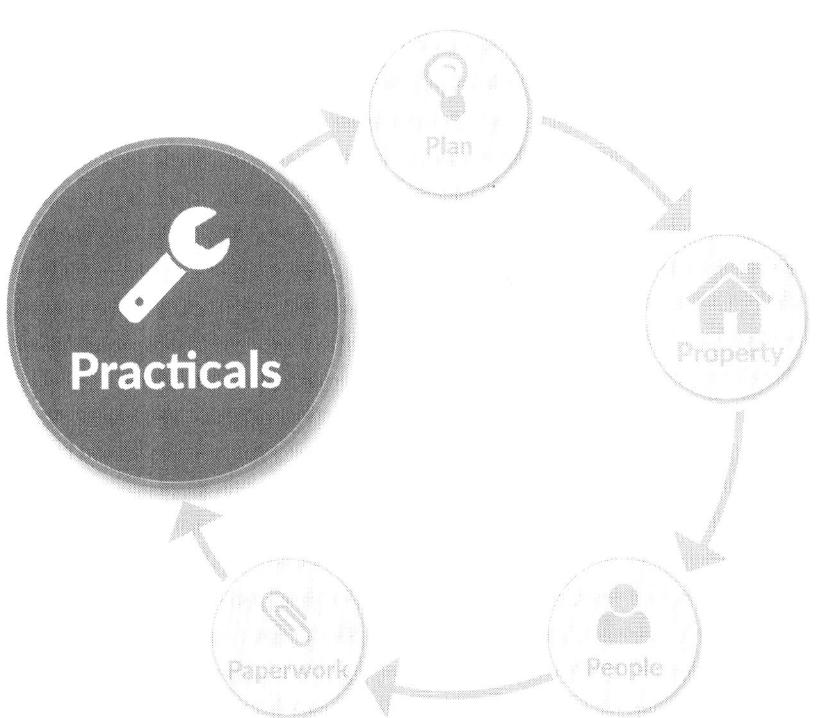

CHAPTER 14

How to stay on top of repairs

In this chapter:

- **Insider tips on inspections, plus how to keep repair costs down**
- **Who does what? And when? The top five maintenance questions answered**
- **How to find – and work with – good tradesmen.**

We've been tenants, too. In the first flat we rented as newlyweds, the boiler once went belly up on a freezing midwinter weekend, leaving us without any heating or hot water. Yet for four days our landlord didn't pick up our calls, emails or SOS signals – so we finally phoned a plumber to save us from frostbite and threatened to deduct the cost from our rent.

As a landlord, you have three good reasons to make prompt repairs:

1. **It keeps the tenants happy.** They'll be more likely to look after your place and stay on. Plus, you've each agreed to keep your end of the bargain: they pay prompt rent, and you make prompt repairs.
2. **It protects your asset.** Today's dripping boiler is tomorrow's £55,000 dry rot bill. Yup, that's a true story.
3. **It's the law.** Many landlords don't know this – like the one who said, 'Why do they need hot water? I shower in cold water.' Fixing that boiler is not optional, and neither is quite a long list of other big repairs (see info below).

What the law says on repairs

By law, the landlord has to keep in good working order:

- The property's structure and exterior, including gutters, drains and pipes
- Heating and hot water
- Basins, sinks, baths and all sanitary fittings
- The water, gas and electricity systems.

You must always give your tenants 24 hours' notice before your tradesman enters, unless it is an emergency. If you refuse to make repairs, tenants can take you to a small claims court for up to £5,000 or – as long as they've written four letters to warn you – fix it themselves and deduct the cost from their rent.

Also, under new revenge eviction laws, you can lose your automatic right to take your house back at the tenancy's end. This applies if your tenant has written to you about the repair but you've failed to respond, and the council has ordered you to fix the issue.

Have you ever booked a cab for a python?

Daniel once needed to book a taxi for a pet python after a leak shorted an Earls Court flat's electricity – and the snake's temperature-controlled terrarium. As these things do, it happened a day before Christmas Eve, when the python's owner spotted water cascading down his walls as he left for the airport. Three hours, 19 phone calls and one bashed-down door later, Daniel finally traced the source to a failed shower connector in the flat four floors above. Bill? £50,000 – which might have been even higher if he hadn't responded so quickly.

The empty third-floor flat, however, suffered extensive floor damage because its selling agent couldn't be bothered to unlock it for the inch-deep water to be mopped up. Though the block's buildings insurer paid out most of the £30,000 in damage, the premiums – and therefore the service charges for all the owners – then shot up. Prompt repairs do pay off.

Be one step ahead with inspections

Proactive maintenance will almost always cost you less than being reactive only once there is serious damage. It also lets you plan ahead to do big projects between tenants and combine works where possible, saving you money. Keep in touch with your tenants so they know you want them to report any issues.

One of the best ways to stay on top of things is through inspections. Build these into your contract so tenants expect them from the start. Doing it more often than every six months, however, can impinge on their right to quietly enjoy their home. Every nine months works well, as you can then see the property in different seasons to catch, say, damp in winter. Also, timing it to be a few months before the contract ends will help you decide if you want to renew.

Be careful to frame the inspection positively when arranging it, so it won't feel like the police checking up. Communicate that it's a chance for the tenants to raise any issues, and that you want to keep the property in good shape. It's their choice whether or not they want to be present.

An inspection doesn't check every last nook and cranny, unlike an inventory report. But look out for:

- **Maintenance problems.** Slow-burners often go unreported, such as a leaking gutter, missing roof tile or damp patches on the walls.

- **Lifestyle issues.** Is there mould in the bathroom or condensation on the walls, suggesting that tenants don't ventilate enough? Do you smell cigarette smoke? If there are filthy extractor fan filters or lots of scuff marks from a buggy, now is the time to warn them that there will be a deduction at the end of the tenancy unless they address the problem.
- **Unauthorised changes.** Have they painted the second bedroom neon pink without asking? Again, remind them to make good or risk their deposit.
- **Contract breaches.** Are there signs of an extra person or unauthorised pet living there, or, worse, that the flat is being used for prostitution or drugs?

As well as inspections, it's a good idea to do some regular scheduled maintenance:

- Clean the gutters once a year to prevent leaks or overflow. (A nesting pigeon blocking the gutter eventually caused dry rot in the flat we rented as newlyweds)
- Sweep working chimneys and flues every two years
- Check the roof every few years for loose tiles (in a house or top-floor flat)
- Replace silicone around baths and showers every few years. This usually gets mouldy, looks bad and eventually leaks
- Repaint rooms every four to eight years.

PRACTICALS

Simple ways to keep repair costs down

When it comes to reactive maintenance, respond quickly to all requests and keep the tenants up to date of progress. As in life, do as you would be done by. Also bear in mind that you have a statutory duty to ensure essentials such as the boiler work. If it breaks and you have to replace it, leaving your tenants without hot water and heating for several days, you may have to put them up elsewhere temporarily.

Keep costs down with these tips:

- **Have a 24/7 emergency number.** A fast response can limit damage – remember the python?
- **Agree a repairs limit.** If you're using an agent, they can then deal quickly with small problems under a set amount.
- **Screen maintenance requests.** This is where a good agent can be invaluable. Work out when to ask the tenant to handle it, go yourself or send a tradesman. 'The oven is not working' often means the timer just needs a reset; if the 'electricity has gone', the tenant might simply have to correct the trip switch. For lost keys you can try to get a locksmith out, but this is a tenant cost.
- **Gather all the information.** Get tenants not just to report a problem ('the washing machine has stopped working'), but to say what caused it ('it sounded like it couldn't spin properly'). Ask for photos of the faults to help tradesmen bring the right equipment. Then, once you've sent someone round, get written confirmation from the tenant that it's fixed.

Tenants say the funniest things

I am writing on behalf of my sink, which is coming away from the wall.

I request permission to remove my drawers in the kitchen.

Will you please send someone to mend the garden path? My wife tripped and fell on it yesterday, and now she is pregnant.

Extracted from real letters to Leicester Council and other housing associations

The top five maintenance questions answered

1. **How much should I budget for maintenance?** Will the boiler conk out in the next week or the next decade? You just don't know. Maintenance costs vary hugely, but set aside 5–10% of your annual rental income for this. A new build flat will likely have fewer costs than a period house. The most important thing, though, is to *set aside something.*

2. **When should I do works?** To prevent territorial irritation, do painting and major works *before the first letting or between tenants* – especially if you want to do it yourself.

3. **My tenant won't let the tradesman in. What can I do?** Write to your tenant that the landlord has a legal right (under Section 11(6) of the Landlord and Tenant Act 1985) to enter the property 'for the purpose of viewing [its] condition and state of repair' at reasonable times of the day and after giving 24 hours' written notice. Keep a log in case there is a dispute. This also applies if the tenant won't let the gas safe engineer in for an annual check.

4. **What is fair to expect my tenant to maintain?** Newbie tenants (and a few spoiled ones) don't know their responsibilities. Legally tenants are stewards of their rented home with a duty to look after it, though they don't have to pay most repair bills. The contract usually lists what the tenant has to do:

    - Take good care of fixtures and fittings
    - Use appliances according to their manuals
    - Put only appropriate items down drains and unblock drains if required
    - Keep the home free from pests
    - Ventilate and keep the property mould-free
    - Not leave the house unattended for more than three to four weeks without telling you
    - Report any serious maintenance issues immediately.

5. **Who maintains the garden?** Though the contract usually says garden maintenance is the tenant's job, in practice it's not that simple. You may have nurtured your garden over years, but your tenants will probably not know their Euphorbia from their Echinacea. If your garden is large or important to you, compromise to ensure your Eden survives. For example:
   - You employ and pay a gardener, but try to include this cost in the rent when negotiating the tenancy terms
   - You do the trees and borders; your tenant does the leaves and lawn
   - Fit an automated sprinkler system so the tenants won't forget to water.

   Include photos of the garden in the inventory, but be aware that you can't hold tenants responsible for every plant that dies. You must also supply the right garden tools. Lastly, be prepared for change – in your few years away, your garden can grow dramatically.

How to find good tradesmen

The last time Daniel tried to change a plug, he fried the cordless phone it powered. Then, when he tried to fix our kitchen light switch, he nearly fried himself. He now gets fried if he doesn't use an expert (writes Martina), which is why he's hired many a tradesman – and can give you pointers on how to do the same.

Tradesmen with both skill and integrity are like hen's teeth (writes Daniel). Once you've found one, pay their invoices promptly and treat them better than you would your own mother.

But how do you pick one in the first place? The usual common-sense rules apply: ask around. A trusted referral beats all. At Swift, Daniel gets references for new suppliers and then gives them a few small jobs to test their skills. Only the good ones get the nod for more work.

In the absence of a recommendation, websites like Which? Trusted Traders (trustedtraders.which.co.uk) and My Builder (mybuilder.com) can help you find a specific trade near you. Some of these sites, though, make it hard for consumers to leave negative reviews. Tradesmen pay to be members, can be charged per lead, and in some cases it's possible to fake glowing reviews – so do your homework on the referral site before you take it seriously.

Should you use a one-man band or a big outfit? Sole traders can be good at their trade but poor at admin, such as quotes, invoices and scheduling. They love the physical side but often hate the paperwork. Plus, the good ones can be too busy to fit you in, especially if your job is not sexy or big enough to interest them.

At large firms the tradesmen can focus on what they do best while support staff deal with the admin, but you'll pay extra for that (and for the fancy vans). Also, you can lose direct contact with the tradesman, which leaves more room for errors. Service can be poor if most of the firm's business is from agents who don't question anything and don't spend their own money.

BIG OR SMALL?	PROS	CONS
Sole traders	▸ Reasonable prices ▸ Personal service ▸ Direct tradesman contact and feedback	▸ Poor admin may waste your time ▸ Slower response if unavailable or off sick with no replacement ▸ Less accountability and recourse to compensation if there are problems
Larger firms	▸ Reliable service ▸ Good admin (usually) ▸ Fast response ▸ Recourse to compensation for any problems	▸ Expensive thanks to high overheads ▸ Lost personal contact with tradesman ▸ Job feedback may be lost if passed via multiple staff

Regardless of size, check that your tradesman or firm has valid public liability insurance and the right professional membership. If they don't, or they dodge your request, walk away. Having this on file will give you recourse to compensation if they are negligent. Sites like My Builder require tradesmen to submit all this, sparing you having to check their credentials yourself.

Be wary of guarantees on workmanship. They are all too easy to wriggle out of: tradesmen may claim the work failed because of an external factor that voids the guarantee. Then it's your word against theirs, and you are not the expert.

Be specific when you instruct a tradesman and do it over email, so there is a paper trail. Include photos, detail on what happened and what exactly they need to fix. Don't just say 'replace the tap'; say which tap in which room, otherwise you might end up with a new tap in the kitchen instead of the bathroom. (Yup, that's another true story.)

Why Joe Schmoe should not be your tradesman

One stormy January night a plumber climbed onto the roof of a block of flats to try and fix a leak into his client's top-floor property. In desperation, he disconnected what looked like an overflowing downpipe. The rain lashed down all night and the next day. But instead of stopping the leak, the plumber's action caused the entire roof's rainwater to plummet down five storeys and crash onto a balcony below. That balcony collapsed under the deluge. The plumber was not qualified to work on a roof, but denied his actions. Due to lack of evidence, the building owners could not claim the £7,000 repair bill on the plumber's insurance. Ouch.

How to stay compliant

If you're digging out a basement (we cover such large projects in Chapter 16 'Make the improvements that matter'), you'd naturally assume that you need permission from the local authority. However, you might not know that much smaller jobs – even fitting a boiler or replacing windows – could need consent, too. There are two sets of hoops to jump through: building control and planning permission. Check which approval your job needs on the government's useful list of common projects at planningportal.gov.uk/permission/commonprojects.

- **Planning permission** is about the principle of whether or not works should go ahead to put up a new building, extend an existing one or change its use. Some projects will fall under permitted development, which means you don't need to seek consent. For example, unless you live in a flat, listed building or conservation area, you can build a rear extension of up to six metres deep on a semi or terraced house (though there are still rules on materials and roof height – it is Britain, after all). But do double-check with your council, as they might have issued a restriction on your area.
- **Building control** checks that the specifics of the works meet standards for safety, sustainability and design. It applies to many jobs, including replacing a roof and electrical work around baths and showers. The tradesman can self-certify that their work complies, as long as they are a competent person, meaning they're a member of a trade body scheme, such as Benchmark for heating or Fensa for windows (check the register at competentperson.co.uk or electricalcompetentperson.co.uk for electrics). They should both notify the council of their work and give you a certificate stating that their work is compliant within 30 days of completion.

If you don't use a competent person but need approval, you must notify your council's building control department or an approved inspector in the private sector before you start work, and pay a fee for an inspection once it's done.

What happens if you don't get building control approval? Without that certificate, you'll have trouble remortgaging or selling your property, as you'll be asked to provide it. Also, the council can order you to put right shoddy work at your expense. In extreme circumstances, you could get an unlimited fine – unsafe work could injure or even kill someone.

Besides consent from the council, you'll also need a licence to alter from the freeholder for many works in a flat. And don't forget about the neighbours: the first time they hear about your project should be when you knock on their door and tell them what you have in mind, not when they get a letter from the council's planning department. That will make them much more amicable when it comes to wrestling over party wall agreements, boundary lines and noisy builders.

Lastly, factor in the time for obtaining all the consents when you plan a project. It can hold things up for months and you don't want your property to sit empty for all that time.

Expect to make repairs and make sure they comply with building control rules. By doing inspections and responding promptly, you will keep tenants happy and costs down. But, hey – you now know how to find a top-notch tradesman to do all this for you, thanks to Daniel's shocking electric skills (pun fully intended).

CHAPTER 15

The 10 most common maintenance problems solved

In this chapter:

- **Low-cost (and no-cost) fixes for your boiler and big appliances**
- **Whose job is it to remove the mould? Plus, savvy advice on leaks, damp and dry rot**
- **Mice, rats, moths, bedbugs...How to tackle Britain's biggest pests.**

The bloody battle of the bedbugs

It began when a south London tenant left an urgent message for Swift. Most tenants think their queries are urgent, even when they're not. But this time the issue turned out to be a nine-month £2,700 battle with bedbugs – one of the worst the pest expert had ever seen. Pests are usually the tenants' responsibility if they start during the tenancy, but in this case the cause turned out to be far more complex.

After failed spray treatments in the upstairs flat, Daniel did his best Poirot impression and deduced that the bloodthirsty critters were crawling up through the floorboards from the flat below to feed on the sleeping tenants.

PRACTICALS

The original source was the downstairs neighbour's boyfriend, who lived nearby. Enter lawyers, the council's public health department and long negotiations – until all three flats were simultaneously heated to 60 degrees, killing all the bugs. The relieved tenants, who understandably had threatened to leave, stayed on; the landlord averted a void and paid only his third of the heat treatment bill.

When the cause or liability is unclear, maintenance problems can be a pain to solve. But – and you can stop shuddering now – many cases are simple, if you know what to look for. In this section we give you the low-down on the 10 most common maintenance issues. Sorry, we can't help with wives who take forever to get ready (writes Daniel). That's a maintenance problem he's still trying to solve.

'The boiler has stopped working'

The problem. You'll get a call, usually on the first freezing weekend in November, because your tenants have no heating – and no hot water, if it's a combi-boiler. Daft as it sounds, it's surprisingly common for the boiler to be switched off, especially if its plug is in a spot that can be confused with a regular socket (see anecdote). Or the boiler may have cut out because the system pressure dropped below a certain level.

None so blind as those who will not see the switch

At 8pm on a Saturday, a new tenant phoned Daniel complaining that there was no hot water in the flat they had just moved into. Could he please send an emergency plumber (at double the usual rate)? Daniel did his usual checks over the phone, but the tenant swore high and low that the boiler was not switched off. Still suspicious, as it had worked when their predecessors moved out days before, he went to check himself – and found the tenants had indeed turned off the boiler by mistake. They just hadn't noticed, as they'd put their fancy new kettle neatly in front of the boiler's power supply.

The solution. To save unnecessary call-out fees, first do a few checks over the phone. This will also help the tenant to fix it faster than waiting for a plumber:

- **Is the boiler on?** Is there a green light somewhere or an LCD display showing that it is definitely on?
- **Is the pressure too low?** Does the gauge read less than 0.5–0.7 bar? Or over 3 bar? Re-pressurising is straightforward for your tenants to do themselves – YouTube has how-to videos for almost all major brands of boilers. It also helps if you have familiarised yourself with that boiler so you can talk your tenants through how it works.
- **Is there an error message?** Googling this may shed light on the fault. But watch out, this may be misleading – leave full diagnosis to a professional.

Boilers do lose pressure over time and it's normal for them to need re-pressurising once or twice a year. If you have to do it more often, though, there may be a leak in the central heating system – call a plumber to investigate.

Should I get boiler insurance?

Some landlords like to take out boiler insurance, often with big household names, but our advice is to steer clear of these products. Swift has seen many cases of incorrect billing, annual premium rises, poor service and – most crucially – no cover when you need it for expensive part replacement.

To avoid ongoing boiler costs, fit a good boiler to start with. The difference between the bottom-end and top-end model is only a few hundred pounds, and much of your cost will be for the labour to install it – that's the same, regardless of the model. Plus, most reputable brands now come with a three- to five-year parts and labour guarantee, giving you peace of mind. An upfront investment in a good boiler will save you not only repair costs, but also the hassle and stress of finding a trustworthy tradesman on short notice.

'The oven/fridge/washing machine is broken'

The problem. Britain throws away half a million washing machines a year, and at least a quarter of them could have been repaired, found the UK Indemand research project. Though it's sadly often cheaper to replace an appliance than repair it, try to fix it when possible – it may save you money and, more importantly, help lower the number of machines in landfill.

Here are some common faults you can fix at low (or no) cost:

- **The washing machine won't drain.** The filter or exit pipe may be blocked. Check the filter at the front of the machine for coins, clips or anything else that may be blocking it. Also check that the exit pipe is clear. YouTube has videos on how to do this for different washing machine makes. Any blockage would be the tenant's bill to pay.
- **The oven doesn't heat up.** If the oven turns on and the grill still works, you only have to replace the oven element.
- **A lot of heat escapes from the oven.** Change the damaged oven seal – this is easy to do yourself.
- **Oven buttons or controls are broken.** Fit new controls, but check the oven seal is not letting heat escape – causing the buttons to melt.

- **The fridge leaks water.** Clear the water exit hole, found at the bottom of the fridge's rear inside wall.
- **The dishwasher doesn't clean properly.** If it leaves bits of dirt, clean out any blocked holes on the rotating arm. Also check that the dishwasher has enough salt and rinse aid.

The solution. Order spare parts for almost any machine from websites such as espares.co.uk, partmaster.co.uk or appliancesparesware-house.co.uk. If you can't fix it yourself, get a specialist appliance repair firm to do the work – they usually charge a fixed fee.

Some faults, however, are not feasible to repair. Scraping noises by the washing machine could mean its drum is damaged, and then it's often cheaper to replace the whole machine. Likewise, if the fridge turns on but no longer cools, the condenser or compressor has usually gone but may be too expensive to fix.

Built-in appliances can be costlier to replace than free-standing ones. They are harder to remove; there are fewer new machines available and they tend to be more expensive; and you may need a carpenter to fit integrated doors. So stick with free-standing where possible.

As with boiler insurance, we'd advise against appliance cover as you can end up paying the whole cost of a new appliance in premiums – only to endure slow response times and painful call-centres.

One last point to mention is that green rules require all appliance retailers to offer a low-cost recycling service for disposing of your old machine. This is usually the cheapest way of getting rid of it.

'Oh dear, we have a leak'

The problem. Leaks can be one of the most difficult and expensive things you may face: difficult because it can be so tricky to establish the source, and expensive because the full extent of the damage can be hidden for a long time. What may seem like a leak from the washing machine upstairs can turn out to be caused by a loose roof tile another floor up, with water travelling all the way down inside the wall.

And the ceiling came tumbling down

In Martina's first London flat share, she and the other tenants reported a damp patch on the bathroom ceiling to the landlord. It seemed to have come from the top-floor water tank. Weeks went by and the owner did nothing, despite their reports that the patch had turned into a drip. Then, one evening as they sat watching TV downstairs, there was an almighty crash. The entire bathroom ceiling, complete with plasterboard and insulation, had collapsed. Thankfully no one was having a bath when it came down.

The solution. We can't emphasise this enough: take leaks seriously and deal with them quickly. Need we remind you of the dripping boiler and the £55,000 dry rot bill?

If you own a leasehold flat, most buildings insurance policies will cover leak damage caused by a source outside your property – even if it was the upstairs neighbour's overflowing bath.

'There's damp everywhere'

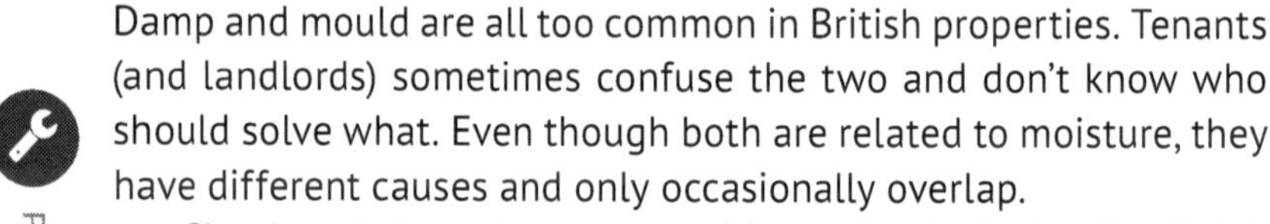

Damp and mould are all too common in British properties. Tenants (and landlords) sometimes confuse the two and don't know who should solve what. Even though both are related to moisture, they have different causes and only occasionally overlap.

Simply put, damp is a structural issue that is the landlord's job to solve. Mould, on the other hand, is usually a condensation issue caused by poor ventilation and is the tenant's responsibility. There are a few exceptions to this rule.

Damp

The problem. Damp affects the structure of the building and can be a result of rising damp (on the ground floor), a plumbing leak from within the property or a leak from an outside source such as a roof, gutter, windowsill or neighbour. The immediate result of damp can be damaged paint and plaster, visible brick salts and moist patches along the wall, and possibly mould growth on these damp patches.

The solution. Damp can cause serious structural damage, such a dry rot (see below), so address any damp as soon as it is found. Sometimes that's easier said than done: it can be very hard to pinpoint the root cause. Damp and leaks into the property from outside are always the landlord's responsibility to resolve. Get an independent damp surveyor to advise, not a damp treatment firm.

Condensation and mould

The problem. Most common in autumn and winter, **condensation** occurs when moist air cools to form water droplets on cold surfaces. Left unchecked, the droplets can cause damage and foster the growth of black mould – which can affect our respiratory health. It happens when three factors combine:

1. **Too much moisture.** Two people at home can produce 12.5 litres of moisture a day through breathing (1.7 litres); cooking and boiling the kettle (3.4 litres); and showering, drying laundry indoors and washing dishes (7.4 litres). There is even more invisible moisture in the air in areas where the water table is close to the ground.
2. **Not enough ventilation.** Circulation helps to replace moist air with drier air from outside. Ironically double-glazing and modern paints make it harder for moist air to escape.
3. **Cold surfaces.** Condensation is worse on windows and external walls, as well as in cold rooms when tenants heat only one room to a high level.

Mould flourishes where there is high moisture, no direct sunlight and warmth – especially in bathrooms. Some properties are far more susceptible to mould than others, for example if they have concrete walls or beams, double-glazing and not much sunlight.

Damp can cause or worsen condensation and mould by raising the moisture levels in a property. However, about 80% of mould is caused by condensation alone.

The solution. Tenants are responsible to remove mould caused by condensation arising from their lifestyle. They can spray the fungus with bleach – Dettol Mould & Mildew Remover is excellent – and wipe away water gathered on window frames and sills.

Then deal with the condensation:

- **Change behaviour.** Ask tenants to reduce moisture: they can dry laundry outside (you can put up a washing line), or in the bathroom with the door shut and the window open – not on the radiators. They can cook with pan lids on and run a bath with cold water first before adding the hot – this cuts steam by 90%. Also, get them to ventilate by opening windows (or at least trickle vents) slightly, even in winter, and to use extractor fans in the bathroom and kitchen. Keeping those two doors closed will also prevent moisture from escaping into the rest of the house.
- **Address any damp or leaks.** It's your responsibility as a landlord to deal with underlying issues.
- **Fit extractors.** If necessary, install and maintain extractor fans in the bathroom and above the hob. In humid rooms with poor ventilation, such as a basement or storeroom, use a dehumidifier to dry out the air. It's also possible to fit a mechanical ventilation system.

Is it mould? Is it damp?

One set of tenants wanted the 'damp' in their bathroom to be repaired, while it was actually mould caused by their own failure to open the window or clean off the fungus. Swift sprayed some Dettol Mould & Mildew Remover and filled the tenants in on its magic. Problem solved.

Another flat, taken on by Swift, had mould in every room. Appalled that the previous agents and tenants had allowed it to become so rampant, Swift cleaned up all the mould, applied anti-mould paint and asked the new tenants to ventilate regularly. Nonetheless the mould returned in autumn and Daniel realised that the concrete structure of this particular property made it so susceptible. The only solution would be a mechanical ventilation system costing thousands of pounds, which the landlord started saving up for. In the meantime the tenants had to keep clearing away mould in the colder months. Problem as yet unsolved.

'What's that mushroom in the corner?'

The problem. One of the biggest risks with leaks is fungal decay. This is how wet rot and dry rot (contrary to its name) start: both are fungi that love moisture and eat away the parts of wood that make timber strong. If you poke the wood with a screwdriver and it sinks in, you have a problem.

Dry rot, the worse of the two, is like kryptonite to Superman, crumbling structural beams and joists into a powdery mess. It loves warm, moist and poorly ventilated areas, usually hidden, such as beneath floorboards, and forms what looks like silvery white roots that travel through masonry and plaster looking for more timber to feed on. Once the spores have taken hold, they can take the shape of a squishy pancake that smells like a mushroom.

Wet rot is more common but stays confined to very damp wood or plaster only. It can manifest as a dark, fern-like pattern on walls or as dark, spongy areas on wood.

The solution. First find and fix the source of the leak, then let it dry out properly – possibly using a dehumidifier and keeping the heating on low. For wet rot you then have to scrape away the damaged areas and refill.

With dry rot, however, you need to remove and treat all the structural elements within 3–6ft of the affected timber. Treating the fungus is not hard, but it becomes expensive because you have to strip out and redecorate such a big area. Buildings insurance usually doesn't cover dry rot as it's seen as avoidable through good maintenance.

'Help! We have creepy crawlies'

One in nine privately rented homes in England has pest problems, estimates the charity Shelter. Whether you're dealing with fleas, wasps or Scrat the squirrel from hell, pest control firms may try to scare you with all the worst-case scenarios if you don't use their services. To escape such pressure, follow these principles when deciding your plan of action:

- **Take a step back.** Be pragmatic and run through all the alternatives rather than jump at an expensive solution that may be overkill.
- **Use a reputable firm.** Not doing so may end up costing you more if you have to re-do treatments. Rentokil (rentokil.co.uk) is one of the best known, but there are many other good firms.
- **Contact your council.** Your local authority will offer pest control services if there is a risk to public health.

It can be upsetting to hear of pests in the home you care about, and naturally you'll want to banish them as soon as possible. But it may be the tenants' responsibility, particularly if their actions have contributed to the infestation. In principle, the landlord is responsible for getting rid of pests that were there at the start of the tenancy, and the tenant for any unwelcome visitors thereafter. However, when the property's structure makes it vulnerable to pests, the landlord does need to get involved, for example by blocking holes that can let mice into a ground-floor flat. Also check what your tenancy agreement says on pests. (Read a useful parliamentary briefing on dealing with pests at tinyurl.com/pests-briefing.)

And now, here's how to deal with the four most common pests in Britain – mothers-in-law excluded.

Mice

The problem. You can tell there are mice by their small black droppings, or you may bump into one – it's normally as shocked as you are (see anecdote). Mice will only live in a property where they can find food, be it in an open bin, low kitchen cupboards or scraps on the floor left by pets or toddlers. They can wriggle through a hole as narrow as a pencil, but are poor climbers who find it hard to access, say, high kitchen cupboards. Ground-floor properties are more susceptible and mice often come inside in autumn or winter when food outside is scarce. They usually don't cause major damage but can gnaw through cables and furnishings. Two mice can become 200 in little more than six months – yes, really – so act fast.

The sad end of Mini Mouse

Martina once opened a kitchen drawer, only to discover a nest with six baby mice of a few days old. Then one hopped out. She (Martina, not the mouse) shrieked and sprang into the air, landing on top of the unsuspecting baby mouse – particularly distressing for all, including Daniel, who had to dispatch the poor mite to mouse heaven.

The solution. Start by removing all food sources. Tell tenants to keep food in sealed containers or high up, get a dustbin with a lid and regularly clean up fallen scraps. Then remove mice via poison or a trap – humane traps are available to catch the mouse but not harm it, so you can release it in a field. Most firms and councils prefer poison as it's easier to set up, but the mouse may then die in an inaccessible place – causing an awful stink.

Rats

The problem. Rats carry nasty diseases, cause major damage chewing through cables, pipes and timber, and contaminate food or water. They're tough, too – Daniel has dealt with rats that swam up through the loo. One rat leaves up to 25,000 droppings a year. Ughhh.

The solution. As with mice, eliminate food and water sources – including bird feeders – otherwise bait won't tempt a well-fed rat. Seal all holes bigger than 15mm where they might gain access. Then put out poison, but keep this out of the reach of children, pets or birds. Or use sealed traps that are child- and pet-friendly: these contain either poison or kill the rodent through a spring mechanism. They also make it easier to dispose of the dead rat – be careful and wear gloves when getting rid of rodent bodies, as they're often infectious.

Moths

The problem. Most of Britain's 2,400 moth species are harmless, but a few have larvae that nibble wool, fur and feathers – damaging carpets, curtains and tenants' clothes (with a penchant for cashmere jumpers). Hanging suits and coats are unlikely targets, as the female moths that lay the eggs can't fly. They pose no health risk to humans.

The solution. Moths flourish in dark, undisturbed spots. If your house becomes affected, moth traps, regular vacuuming (with a good vacuum cleaner, including under all furniture, and emptying the contents outside) and possibly a carpet steam clean can oust the problem. For a more serious infestation, you may need a spray treatment from a pest-control firm, which almost always does the trick. In extreme cases, try a heat treatment, but this is expensive and very seldom necessary. You can also simply fit synthetic carpets (or no carpets) – they're far too bourgeois for the larvae's refined palate.

Bedbugs

The problem. From nymph to adult, all stages of bedbugs feed on human blood every 10 or so days, but they can go for months without a meal. They don't carry diseases but their bites can cause allergic reactions, sleeplessness and stress. They can enter your property as stowaways picked up at a hotel abroad or hidden in the cracks of that vintage chest of drawers bought on eBay. Resistant to insecticide, tiny and nocturnal, they can be harder to eradicate than Bruce Willis on a bad day.

The solution. To quell a minor invasion, seal cracks and crevices, such as in bed frames, skirting boards and floorboards. Tell tenants to launder and tumble-dry on high heat, vacuum frequently and reduce clutter. For large infestations, however, you may need an expert to spray pesticide or, worst case, heat the entire property to 60 degrees (see earlier anecdote). Kill 'em dead!

We could go on about ants, cockroaches, woodworm and endless nasties, but we think that's quite enough about pests. Time to move on to less creepy topics – how about the genteel world of Farrow & Ball?

CHAPTER 16

Make the improvements that matter

In this chapter:

- **Five refurbs that will boost your let, plus five extensions that will up your sale**
- **Trade secrets to get the best out of your builder (and how to vet them, too)**
- **Three dust-free ways to add value: get planning consent, extend your lease or buy the freehold.**

Before you start oohing and aahing over hand-painted kitchens and copper baths on Houzz.co.uk, pause and ask whether you should renovate at all. There's no doubt that the right refurb can add value, but the reality of building works is far from romantic. It involves lots of dust, almost as many decisions and double the stress, time and money you'd expect. Don't do it lightly.

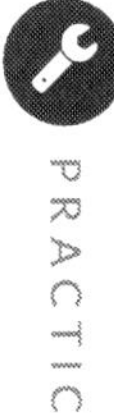

Revisit your goals for your property (see Chapter 1 'How to avoid the No.1 landlord mistake'): whatever you do should tie in with them. Plus, it should make more money than it costs – lost sleep and lost rent included. That new kitchen or bathroom will take years to recoup through raised rent, but there may still be good reasons to go ahead, such as to:

- Increase the sale price if you'd like to sell soon
- Up the property standard so it attracts better tenants and rents faster

- Add a bedroom – done properly, this will add both rental and sales value
- Tackle a big maintenance problem
- Maximise the property's potential, raising both the rent and the long-term capital value.

For the record, these are not good reasons to renovate:

- Everyone in the street has done a loft conversion, so we should too
- I've always wanted that dream bathroom
- The kitchen is perfectly functional, but so eighties
- Wouldn't it be nice to have more natural light?

When it comes to spec for rental properties, there are two big newbie mistakes. The first is to choose finishes of the same standard that you'd have liked. Look at comparable 'let agreed' properties on Rightmove and Zoopla and use their finishes as a guide. For all except top-end rentals, durability and functionality are all that matter. Tenants won't fork out for bespoke built-in wardrobes or marble fireplaces. To them, the most important factors are location, rent and space – though it's about having just enough space for their needs, unlike homeowners who want as much space as possible. Only 15% of private tenants have two or more spare bedrooms, compared to almost 50% of people who own their homes, census data shows.

And the second mistake? That's easy – don't impose your taste. Keep walls white, floors neutral and ceilings clear of taxidermy chandeliers, however trendy they may seem. Most tenants simply want clean and bright.

Pardon the sermon, but too many people get this spectacularly wrong. When deciding if and how to do a refurb, do it with the mindset of an investor – not a homeowner. Unless, of course, you're planning to move back or sell soon, in which case your preferences or those of your target buyer become the most important.

Five improvements to boost your let...

If you want to let out your property long-term, these five improvements – each possible for under £10,000, if not much less – will help you find good tenants quickly and possibly up your rent. Done well, they will also add to an eventual sale price. However, do your homework first and get advice from a good local agent on which improvements will make a difference in your market.

These works will make the property uninhabitable for weeks, so do them between tenancies or, at a push, when your tenant is away – and always leave margin for overrun.

Reconfigure the layout

The cost: from £1,200 to knock through a non-structural wall and make good; more if you have to level uneven floors or move radiators.

The gain: up to 10%, depending on how poky rooms were before.

Making the most of your floorplan can add value at a fraction of what an extension would cost. Knock out a wall to make the kitchen open-plan – that can appeal to renters and buyers alike, as long as it's in balance with the rest of the home. In two-bedroom urban flats, balance the bedrooms with one another so they are similar sized – ideally both en suite – to attract professional sharers. Incorporate wasted hallways into rooms and create lots of storage.

Update the kitchen

The cost: from £3,500–the sky is the limit.

The gain: around 5%.

The price bracket of the kitchen should match that of the house. A £5,000 laminate special in a £1m house will drag down the value of the whole place. Equally, it's overkill to fit handmade cabinets worth £20,000 in a £200,000 flat. The right kitchen is key to get feet through the door but don't expect it to put much money in your pocket – it will cost about as much as it will add in sales value. To recoup your outlay in increased rent, you'd have to hold on to your property for at least five years.

The savvy investor's top 10 kitchen tips

1. Do you need a whole new kitchen? It's far cheaper to keep units and only change cupboard doors and handles, plus perhaps a new worktop
2. Large suppliers, including B&Q, Ikea, Howdens, Magnet and Homebase, offer a useful free kitchen planning service to help you plan the space
3. Use your own fitter. The fitting service of major suppliers is outsourced and can be patchy and expensive
4. Avoid finishes that could easily mark (white surfaces) or that require regular maintenance (wooden worktops)
5. Double-check that spaces are big enough for the appliances you want to install. (A standard appliance is 60cm wide and about 60cm deep)
6. Include a dishwasher if possible – even a slimline one – as tenants increasingly ask for this
7. Choose a fridge proportionate to the number of bedrooms and with a decent-sized freezer
8. While built-in appliances look sleek, they're more expensive to maintain: there is much less choice in replacement machines and fitting the built-in doors can be tricky
9. Gas hobs are popular but need an annual gas safety check and add risk, albeit small. Induction hobs are safer and won't require such checks
10. In narrow or galley kitchens make sure there is enough space for cabinet or appliance doors to open fully.

Redo the bathroom

The cost: £1,000–£10,000+

The gain: 0–5%.

Materials for a bathroom makeover aren't particularly expensive – you can pick up a whole suite under £1,000 – but labour, especially tiling, pushes up costs. Don't spend on designer taps or top-of-the-range tiling; you'll never get that money back. Instead of a shower over a bath, which often leaks, consider a walk-in shower. Unless your target tenants are families, this will add some wow factor and is cheaper to maintain.

Lay wooden floors

The cost: from £500 for a small room without tricky corners.

The gain: not much, if any.

Wooden floors will help you let or sell faster, but not necessarily for more rent. However, consider laying them when you have to take up carpets anyway, for example after you've had moths. Or it may cost less to sand and treat your original timber floorboards, if they are in good nick. For flats, check the lease: wooden floors may be banned to limit noise. If they are allowed, fitting good soundproof underlay will usually prevent problems with the neighbours below.

Upgrade the energy efficiency

The cost: from around £150 to fit six LED downlights; £300 to insulate a loft.

The gain: you'll avoid a poor rating that puts people off.

Tenants (and buyers) are more aware of energy efficiency and will think twice before taking a property with the low ratings of E, F or G on its energy performance certificate (EPC). Indeed, from April 2018 it will be illegal to let out an F- or G-rated home on a new tenancy, though there are ways around this (see Chapter 7 'Tick the legal boxes'). Smart tenants will ask questions about heating bills for D-rated properties; an A to C rating won't put anyone off – but won't push up your price either. If you have a poorly rated property, and especially if you have great tenants who complain about astronomical bills, you may want to improve the energy efficiency.

Your EPC will suggest some generic changes, but this is no substitute for expert advice from a good specialist such as Enhabit (enhabit.uk.com). Possible steps include:

- Replace bulbs and light fittings with energy efficient LEDs
- Install double-glazing (you have to anyway when replacing most windows)
- Insulate the loft (for houses and top-floor flats)
- Fit an efficient gas combination boiler and get rid of all tanks that heat and store excess hot water.

...and five improvements to up your sale

At more than £10,000 each, you'll never recoup these five improvements in rent alone. Do them only to increase the value of your property ahead of a sale.

Always follow the two golden rules: don't overdevelop for your area – if all the houses in your street sell for £300,000, there's a ceiling on what you could charge for yours, even if you added a monster basement with a hydrotherapy spa. And don't overdevelop for your space: balance living and sleeping areas. A cavernous open-plan entertainment space will have limited appeal if there is just one bedroom.

Not all works add value. Conservatories often detract, outdoor pools add none and buyers see those standalone garden rooms as a fantastic extra but not one they'd pay more for.

So, which improvements are worth it? We can't tell you, but a local estate agent can. They will know how much more – if anything – buyers would pay for the following. As a very rough starting point, however, we'll throw in a few ballpark figures.

Convert the loft

The cost: £50,000–£100,000

The gain: as much as 20%.

Adding a double bedroom and an extra bathroom in the loft can add more than a fifth to the value of a three-bedroom one-bathroom house, found research by Nationwide Building Society. This is usually the cheapest type of extension, as you're not digging any new foundations. It's not very disruptive, either: much of the work can be done from outside. To pay off, access to the loft must be easy (not via another bedroom or a ladder) and the ceiling must still be high enough to stand up after the floor has been raised to strengthen the joists.

Extend to the side

The cost: £30,000–£80,000

The gain: 10–20% in city locations.

Filling in the side return – the narrow strip of garden next to the galley kitchen – doesn't add that much floor space but can transform your kitchen/living room into a much more usable space that flows into the garden. It can get expensive, though, if you need to install steel beams. For a lower-cost dose of wow, you could simply flip the room around, moving the kitchen to run along an interior wall, and fitting big glass doors to the garden at the other end.

Create a roof terrace

The cost: from £15,000

The gain: 12% in inner London.

Adding a roof terrace is a cost-effective way to add value, especially to two- and three-bedroom flats. In the best parts of central London, such as Chelsea, it could raise the price by as much as 25% over that of an identical flat without outside space. You will, however, need to buy the roof demise and get consent from the freeholder.

Convert the garage

The cost: £10,000–£20,000

The gain: multiply the garage's square footage by the local price per square foot.

Nine in ten British garages don't house a car. Turf out the stored goods and turn it into a study, playroom, TV room or extra bedroom if it adjoins the house and the floorplan allows.

Dig a basement

The cost: £150,000–£500,000

The gain: multiply the extra square footage by the local price per square foot.

At around £500 per sq ft, basements are the most expensive form of extension. They are also the most invasive, affecting the structure of the whole building – so only worth it in prime London areas and after careful thought.

How to work with builders

When you're letting out your home, time really is money – every day the work drags on is another day without rent. A professional will do it faster than you could (unless you happen to be a pro, of course). Only do the work yourself if the sum of the lost rent and the cost of your time is still cheaper than paying a builder.

Sadly, few projects are straightforward – even if your brilliant builder has a flying start and you tell yourself, 'It'll be different with us.' Martina interviews property owners for a living, yet can count on the fingers of one hand those who've had works without worries – whether that's weather, delayed supplies or a can of worms uncovered along the way.

Cowboy pushes terrace price through the roof

Their new roof terrace would be easy-peasy, promised the first company Shelley and Ryan had hired: just three weeks, £10,000 and Bob-the-builder's your uncle. In the end it took eleven months, £18,000, two building companies and one bespoke steel post that crashed through the downstairs neighbour's skylight – narrowly missing her nine-year-old son. Thankfully, the terrace did add £60,000 in value to the two-bedroom London flat.

Five checks for choosing a builder

As ever, a recommendation tops all. If a friend's builder finished on budget with a month to spare, you're on to a winner. Failing that – as for finding a tradesman – try Which? Trusted Traders (trustedtraders.which.co.uk) and My Builder (mybuilder.com).

Good builders are busy, so plan ahead – you may have to wait a few months before they can start. Even if a builder comes recommended, Daniel does a few extra checks:

1. **Previous clients.** Always ask to speak to at least two, preferably recent ones. If the builder can't provide these references, don't use them.
2. **Trade bodies.** Do they belong to any? Check with the trade bodies to verify their membership is up to date.
3. **Company records.** If they are run as a company, check that the company exists and that its regulatory filings are up to date at Companies House.
4. **Insurance.** Their public liability insurance must be valid.
5. **Google them.** Always search online for the name of both the company and its owner. Apart from reviews – positive or

negative – you may catch out, as Daniel has done, a builder who works as a company but also moonlights for cash-in-hand jobs to avoid tax.

Price alone should never be the key driver for which builder you choose: prices can change during the project – and less scrupulous builders deliberately inflate prices for extras that were not included from the start.

Ten ways to get the best from your builder

We won't patronise you with advice to make your builder cups of tea (though that helps). The key to getting the best out of them is to be clear upfront on scope and costs:

1. **Make design choices early.** Decide exactly what you want to do before the builders arrive and don't change your mind half way through the project. Research your chosen finishes in good time – they can take a long time to arrive or be out of stock just when you need them, holding up the whole build.
2. **Write a clear brief.** Add as much detail as possible. If you leave your builder to fill in the gaps, you can't blame them for an end result you dislike.
3. **Check the quote.** Insist on a fixed-price quote, rather than one based on how long the job takes, so your builder won't have any incentive to drag things out. Ask that they break it down into labour and materials. Daniel then checks what it does and doesn't include – for example, how many days for each trade at which rate. He usually leaves it to the builder to source basic materials as they get trade discounts and, even if they mark it up to reflect their time ferrying it around, it saves him doing it.
4. **Learn from others.** Run ballpark quotes by forums for like-minded property owners (thepropertyhub.net, propertytribes.com, landlordzone.co.uk). They can also offer pearls of wisdom on what to look out for during a refurb, getting past the planners and keeping your tenants on side.

5. **Use an architect.** For a major project, we'd strongly encourage hiring an architect at least to draw up the plans (this can cost under £1,000; find an architect at architecture.com or via the matchmaker architectsrepublic.com). Their creative input and insight into the planning process will help you make the most of your property.
6. **Budget 20% for contingency.** This is pessimistic, but will allow for valid but unforeseen costs (which don't include succumbing to the £250 kitchen tap just because the £50 one isn't that chic after all). The worst thing that can happen is that you run out of cash after the builders have made a mess of the place, but before they've put it right again.
7. **Manage time.** Double whatever timescale your builder gives you to get a realistic picture of how long it will take. You will likely lose rental income for the whole time, so use a contract with penalty clauses for delays – a good builder will agree to this. The Federation of Master Builders has a template contract where you can fill in the blanks (home-extension.co.uk/fmbcontract.pdf). Even so, factor in contingency time. If it absolutely has to be done in two months, tell everybody from the start that they have one month to finish.
8. **Monitor often.** Visit the site daily or every few days. If you don't have the time or skillset, hire a project manager (or your architect) to do this – but even then you still need to be on the phone every day. There are constant decisions to make: where exactly to place lights, how high the counter should be, which way the door should open...They're easy to get right during the build, but hard to fix afterwards. Keeping tabs will avoid costly mistakes and show your builder that they can't quietly fade out to start work elsewhere.
9. **Stagger payments.** Agree at the start when you'll make payments. Most builders expect a partial sum upfront for materials, but keep this small. Then it's normal to make staged payments once each phase is complete.

10. **Withhold 25% until after snagging.** At the end of the project, run through the finished work and make a 'snag list' of any small items that need to be addressed. Be firm and – despite inevitable protests – don't pay the final 25% until all the snags are fixed. Once you've made the bulk of your payments, you have little power to hold your builder to account.

Other ways to add value

Apart from refurbs and extensions, a third way to add value is through solving a legal problem that restricts the sale price, such as a short lease. This won't help you let your property, but it could pay off handsomely when it comes to selling.

Get planning permission

If you can't afford an extension or conversion, you can still add value by getting planning permission for it. Around £2,500 should cover a survey, drawings and the official processing for a standard project. That will remove doubt from a buyer's mind and can significantly raise your property's value.

Extend your lease

Extending a short lease is essential if you want to protect your flat's value. England and Wales have more than 4 million leasehold flats, with leases granted for long periods – often 125 years, but they can be as long as 999 years. It means you 'rent' the property for a very long time, but when the lease expires you have to hand the keys to the building's owner, called the freeholder.

The shorter the lease, the more expensive it is to renew it – so the lower the price of the flat. Once a lease dips below 80 years, the renewal cost starts to rocket exponentially. When it gets to around 60 years, the flat becomes virtually unmortgageable and very hard to sell. So don't delay; extend as soon as possible.

A quick guide to lease extensions

Who can extend? If you've owned a flat for two or more years, you have a legal right to extend the lease for at least 90 years at a fair market rate.

When should I extend? Start looking into extending your lease when it has 83 years left. Move quickly if it's below 80 years; beneath 60 years you'll need expert legal advice.

How much will it cost? The Leasehold Advisory Service's calculator gives a broad steer (lease-advice.org.uk/calculator), but working out the value is complex and subject to negotiation. Unless it's only a few thousand pounds, hire a valuation surveyor with a good grasp of the local property market to calculate it for you (from around £500). Also factor in legal fees (see below).

How do I extend my lease? First speak to your freeholder informally. They might accept your offer straight off. If not, you'll have to pay for a valuation surveyor and a solicitor. By law, you usually have to pay the freeholder's legal fees. You then make a formal offer and negotiate the price. If you can't agree, you'll have to apply to the First-tier Tribunal.

How long does all this take? Three months to a year; longer if it goes to tribunal.

What should I look out for? Some firms invest in thousands of freeholds, collect the ground rent and pray that you let your lease drop below 80 years – and then they rake in the cash. Beware, too, of freehold companies who offer a lower extension fee but with a ground rent that rises over time, as it will ultimately devalue the property. Go armed with an experienced leasehold solicitor and surveyor on your side.

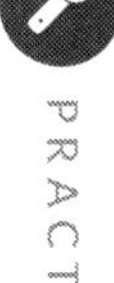

What if I can't afford to extend but want to sell? Make the lease extension part of the sale, so the buyer won't have to wait for two years until they have the right to extend. You can serve a renewal notice on the freeholder after exchange of contracts, but before the sale completes. The buyer can get a mortgage conditional to this.

What happens once I've extended my lease? You'll still have to pay the freeholder the usual service charges but your ground rent should fall to a symbolic yet worthless peppercorn rent. At one block of flats in Manchester, where the 250-year lease was renewed in 2013, the payment dropped to the token of: 'One pound of Lancashire cheese, a pint of locally produced beer, one locally produced loaf of bread and one farm free range organic chicken.' A healthy profit after all.

Buy the freehold

It could be worth clubbing together with fellow flat-owners in your building to buy out the freeholder in a process called enfranchisement, and then extend the leases to 999 years for free. In theory, this makes you masters of your own destiny when it comes to running the building, but in practice it brings the problem of making decisions by committee.

PRACTICALS

To exercise your right to buy the freehold, at least 50% of the flat owners must agree to proceed and you have to meet certain legal conditions. As a rough rule of thumb, the price of a share of the freehold for one flat equates to extending its lease by 90 years. You'll also need to fork out for the valuation (about £4,000 for a block of five flats), plus your own and the freeholder's legal fees. This is a complex area of law, so get expert advice. Find specialist solicitors via the Leasehold Advisory Service (lease-advice.org); read a full guide at moneysavingexpert.com/mortgages/buy-freehold-right-to-manage.

Dead firm gives studio new lease of life

Adam, a client of Swift, snapped up a studio flat in west London at the bargain price of £125,000 at auction after the owner had died. The place had to be gutted, but he'd done that before. What he didn't realise, however, was that it had only 64 years left on the lease – and the company that owned the building's freehold, in which all the other flat owners held shares, had collapsed after years of mismanagement. To renew the lease became a four-year ordeal in which he had to round up the apathetic owners, restore the company and negotiate his extension price. It was worth it in the end: after he'd spent £30,000 on the lease and refurb, the flat was valued at £250,000.

With your only costs being time and legal fees, steps like extending the lease or getting planning consent can be very lucrative indeed. But whether you want to add value on paper or in bricks, first ask yourself why you want to do it. Does it tie in with your long-term property goal? Only go ahead if your answer is yes.

Part 6
Conclusion

CHAPTER 17

How to buy more... and build a portfolio

In this chapter:

- **Avoid the biggest newbie mistake: get finance in place upfront**
- **How to build a portfolio on limited funds. Plus, what BMV is (and isn't)**
- **Where to look for deals – and what to look out for**
- **The key questions to ask when buying off-plan, leasehold or with tenants.**

As an accidental landlord, you probably didn't pick your first property with renting in mind. To make a success of letting it, you've had to make the best of what you'd got. However, if you buy more, you have the luxury of choice. This time round, you can buy as an investor – not an owner.

You now have one big advantage over other beginners: you already have a property investment. That has given you not only the experience of running it, but also the means towards buying more. If you're smart, you could even build a portfolio on the back of it. In this section, we arm you with the knowhow to choose wisely – and the vision to think beyond that next purchase.

But first we need to revisit the big questions we asked at the start of this property investment journey. Before you read any further, work through the goal exercise in Chapter 1 'How to avoid the No1 landlord mistake': are you investing so you can live in a hammock, launch a business, leave your kids a nest egg or retire in comfort? Has your big why changed? Should you shift your target between long-term price growth and monthly rental income, and how much of each do you need? It is crucial to know where you're going, otherwise you may end up with a property that won't help you to get there.

Perhaps even bigger than these is one other question to think about: the ethics of being a buy-to-let owner. In a country where many a renter despairs of ever owning their home, you are privileged enough to be buying your next investment property. The price growth from which you stand to benefit is driven by the chronic shortage of homes, which means that your gains are paid for by those less wealthy. The point is this: with our power comes responsibility. Our actions affect not only our properties, but also the communities around them and our tenants' lives – sometimes greatly. We have a duty of care well beyond legal duties in how we exercise this influence.

Is your property goal realistic?

To have realistic expectations of what you can achieve, consider:

- **Money.** How much capital do you have?
- **Timeframe.** By when do you want to achieve your goal? Do you plan to hold the property for many years, or sell soon?
- **Effort.** How much time do you have? Are you prepared to do any works?
- **Risk appetite.** Are you prepared to take on more risk – in, say, an up-and-coming area or a shared multi-let – in return for more rewards?

These factors interact: if you have less of one, you'll need more of the rest. For example, you could earn £4,000 a month from property within a year if you have £1m in capital, or work 80 hours a week to buy, do up and sell wrecks. Otherwise it would take you close to a decade to get there – possibly less if you let your properties room by room to sharers, which makes more money but takes more effort.

Income goal trumps period dream

Sam's pension would not be enough for her to retire on, so she decided to invest in a buy-to-let flat that would give her a balance between rental income and price growth. Though she first looked at period homes like her own Victorian flat, she realised the rent would be too low to give her the income she wanted. She settled on a nearby flat in a small modern (but not brand new) block which would have lower running costs. Knowing her goal helped her to make the right choice.

Get finance in place

After setting your property goal, your next step is to sort out financing. Don't leave this for last – that's one of the biggest newbie mistakes. Backing out of a deal because you can't borrow enough will waste your time and destroy your credibility with estate agents.

Five ways to raise capital

To cover your deposit, purchase fees and refurb costs, you could:

1. **Save.** That's the obvious answer. Avoid lifestyle inflation and put your cash aside instead.
2. **Remortgage.** If your property has risen in value – because you've improved it or the market has gone up – you can withdraw that equity tax-free by borrowing against the new value. However, the amount you can take out will be capped by either the property's rental value (if you're taking out a new buy-to-let loan on your rental property) or your own income (if you're borrowing against your main home). Also, beware your cash flow: more debt means higher interest payments. If you barely break even or make a monthly loss, you won't be able to ride out problems and could lose the property alto-

gether. Lastly, watch out for hefty repayment penalties from your current lender.

3. **Sell.** A good option if your old property is not meeting your goals anymore, but selling may land you with a fat capital gains tax bill.
4. **Pension.** Under new rules, over-55s can now withdraw all or part of their pension pot and use the money as they please – including on buy-to-let. However, this involves far more work, stress and risk than buying an annuity that pays you a monthly income. You may also face a triple whammy of tax that you would not have to pay if you left the funds in your pension: income tax, capital gains tax and inheritance tax. Get expert tax advice before taking this route.
5. **Joint venture.** Team up with a family member or friend who has the cash, ideally in the form of a loan on which you offer them a fixed interest rate (typically 6%–12% a year). You could split the profits, with them putting up the money and you doing the work, or you could both put in equal amounts and share the rewards. No matter how close you are, *always draw up a declaration of trust* that says who will invest how much, do which tasks and against what security. Also state what happens if things go well – and if they don't.

Where to borrow the rest

Unless you're a cash buyer, in most cases you'll need a buy-to-let mortgage to fund your property. Unlike a residential mortgage, this is pegged to how much the property rents for – not your earnings. For this you will need a deposit of at least 25% and the rent has to cover 125%-145% of the mortgage payments to allow for empty periods and interest rate rises. You can't assume that, because you have a deposit, you'll get a mortgage: lenders will look at the rental valuation plus a raft of other requirements. (See Chapter 3 'Switch to the right mortgage and insurance' for all you need to know about buy-to-let mortgages.)

However, a mortgage is not the right tool for flips and auctions. It takes too long to arrange for auction purchases, where you have to pay all the funds within 28 days. And lenders see mortgages as long-term finance – they don't like using them for short-term flips, where you buy to sell quickly without letting.

So, what should you use? Apart from cash, your only option is bridging finance. That's quick to arrange and can fund up to 70% of the purchase price, even on homes that are unmortgageable because there's no working kitchen or bathroom. If you're buying for a bargain price, you can take out bridging finance based on the full market value of the property – giving you extra money to fund a refurb.

But what's the catch? You guessed it: bridging will cost you. Around 0.75%–1.5% per month, to be precise, plus steep fees and skyrocketing interest rates at the end of the loan term. Also, watch out for the 'six-month rule': most lenders won't let you refinance a property in fewer than six months, even if you're going from bridging finance to a mortgage. So plan to have a bridging loan for at least eight months, which gives you enough time to arrange a mortgage once the first six months are up.

Buy with a portfolio in mind

If you want to build a portfolio, you have to think beyond your next purchase. By buying smartly, you can position yourself so that you can extract most of the cash sunk into this deal to reuse it for the next one.

How? The key is to create equity. You can do this in one of two ways (or, more likely, a combination of these two ways):

1. **Buy below market value (BMV).** Paying less than what the property is really worth creates equity out of thin air.
2. **Buy where you can add value.** Look for a property where you can extend, do a major refurb or solve a legal problem such as a short lease that limits its value.

Your next step is to refinance to tap into that equity. If you've only bought BMV, you'll have to wait one to two years to do so, otherwise the lender's surveyor will value your property too close to the bargain price you paid for it. If you've added value as well, you can remortgage sooner – but no sooner than six months, as we've seen above. Also, if you plan to refinance after such a short period, you'll need to take out a bridging loan instead of a buy-to-let mortgage for the initial period.

Buy below market value

Though you may think that the market value is simply whatever a buyer is willing to pay, the price can vary depending on either party's circumstances. For example, two identical flats on the same street can sell for vastly different prices if one is marketed by a hapless agent who forgets to upload any photos to Zoopla, while the other is subject to a bidding war between three smitten buyers.

So, it is possible to buy below market value in the sense that you can pay a lower price than what would have applied in a different situation. However, be sceptical about any sale advertised as a BMV opportunity – you may be dealing with thieves in suits. *It's not BMV if the true market value is lower than they say.* Back to our identical flats: a hidden reason could repress one's value, for instance a nightmare neighbour, a short lease or a looming major works bill. It's your job to work out why it's so cheap: is the owner just getting desperate, or is there something wrong?

How to assess market value

To assess what a property is really worth, forget the asking price and pretend that you're a surveyor who objectively has to determine its market value. Start by finding similar homes nearby that sold recently. Access Land Registry data on sold property values by searching under 'House Prices' on Rightmove and Zoopla within ¼ mile of your postcode (or ½ mile if there are not enough results). Then click in and out of results to find properties of the same size, layout and spec. Ignore the outliers priced unusually high or low, and you'll soon spot a pattern of what the average price is.

You could also browse for sale properties, but bear in mind that these are asking prices – not actual sale prices. For extra peace of mind, a valuation survey by Hometrack (hometrack.com) does all this electronically for about £20. Make deductions for any hidden flaws such as that short lease or major works bill.

Then consider: does the price work for you? By this we don't only mean that you should be able to afford it. It must also suit your goal. Think back to the start of this book: if you are after a specific yield to get a set amount of rental income, this property might not be the right one for you – even if it's sold at a discount.

Always pay the lower of these two prices: what it's really worth (the market value) and what it's worth to you (the price that suits your strategy).

Buy to add value

When buying a property to do up, extend or solve a legal problem for, the asking price has nothing to do with how much you should pay. To work out what that is, work backwards from the price at which you would be able to sell, and be pessimistic in your estimate. Then, deduct all your costs – plus another 10% of that for contingency – and a 20% margin to reward yourself for all your hard work. Pay no more than this:

Maximum purchase price = price you can sell for – costs – your profit margin

This equation is what separates the winners from the wannabes. All too often amateurs knock 10% off the asking price and think they've got a great deal – only to overspend on a swish glass kitchen extension and sell for a loss. By using the formula above, you'll do it like a pro.

There's one more thing: buy in an area where there is strong demand from owner-occupiers, and do to the property just what would appeal to them. Ultimately you want a bidding war between love-struck buyers – and that will only happen when people are buying a home to live in, not to invest in. To check demand, ask several local agents how long properties stay on the market before they sell, and how many viewings that takes on average. You can also check the average sale listing age on Rightmove and Zoopla, but that data is often distorted by agents who forget to take down listings or de-list and re-list the same property several times.

For the nitty gritty on how to tackle refurbs, extensions and legal solutions, see Chapter 16 'Make the improvements that matter'.

Where to look for deals

Your instinct may be to look in the immediate area where you live, but don't let that blinker you. Londoners often fall into this trap, yet the capital is not alone in the buy-to-let universe: people north of the Watford Gap need houses, too. And they do have jobs. Some even like flat whites.

Though your local knowledge and connections are valuable, your area may not be right for your investment goals – looking within a 45-minute radius could yield better results. That said, it's worth buying close to any existing properties you own so you can use the same trusted local suppliers or lettings agent.

No matter what the property press tells you, forget about finding the ultimate hotspot. It's far more important that the numbers of the specific deal stack up, and that the area has the right fundamentals. For the property to both let and sell easily, people must want to live there. That means there should be access to jobs, transport and shops within 10 minutes, good schools and a park nearby.

It would also help if:

- Current transport links mean you could easily get there yourself
- You have friends or family in the area – they can be the start of your local network and insider knowledge
- You know the area from having lived there before
- You're copying others who've successfully invested there
- You see a strong investment story with regeneration, gentrification or new transport links. Though prices will start rising once a new rail link has been announced, the full growth will only kick in once the wheels have started rolling. Take Crossrail in west London: a banker will only buy in Chiswick, near Acton Main Line station, once the trains open in 2018 to cut journey times into the City from 45 to 16 minutes.

How do you narrow it down from 'Bristol's a bright idea' to 'let's look along the waterside in hip Hotwells'? First speak to a local letting agent or your old friend from uni who's lived there all her life. Failing that, here's how Martina researches areas she has to write about without having been there: start with googling phrases like 'areas in [city]' or '[area] regeneration'. Forums like Mumsnet and area guides in newspapers will give you a feel for the parts to home in on or avoid. Look at the area on a map and see where it is relative to transport links, employment hubs, shops and universities (if you're targeting students).

Then you need an idea of costs. Search on Home.co.uk for prices and rents in the first part of the postcode. That will give you a very rough idea of what the average homes there sell and let for. To drill down in more detail, fire up Rightmove or Zoopla and draw the exact area you're interested in, then click in and out of properties in the map view to look for trends. Combine this with Google Street View and you'll start to form a surprisingly clear picture of the best and worst streets, and whether the price range is in your budget. Ahead of any viewings, it's worth driving or cycling around the area to fine-tune your research.

Notting Hill neighbour turns into star performer

When we were looking for medium-term capital growth to help us buy a bigger family house, we chose a one-bedroom period flat with a garden in Maida Hill – a relatively undervalued pocket of northwest London. Surrounded by pricy Notting Hill, St John's Wood and Queens Park, this slightly scruffy area was on the cusp of gentrification with skips, shutters and independent shops springing up. The flat itself was on one of the prettiest streets, a five-minute walk from the Tube station and two blocks from a swish new-build development where an M&S Simply Food would open.

Even better, we could create a second bedroom without any building works. All we did was to put a double bed in the former front living room, and remove a few cabinets from the rear kitchen/diner – making space for sofas in this open-plan room. That meant we could charge almost £200 a month more in rent. Within a year, the flat rose in value by about £100,000. It pays to choose well.

How to look for deals

Estate agents

Don't get fixated on finding an off-market sale – you often end up paying extra for that exclusivity. The most common way to find good deals is more mundane: through an estate agent.

Of course you want to be a good agent's BFF, first to hear of any red-hot offers, but that's unlikely. They've heard a hundred others vow that they're 'cash buyers' who can 'move fast'. Until they know that you're the real deal, try these tactics:

- **Bad agents are good for you.** That flat with the single fuzzy smartphone snap and the typos in the Rightmove advert is the one to ring up about first. The advert will put off most owner-occupiers and plenty of lazy investors. Even better, find a sale listed in the local newspaper only – not on the big portals – and you know you won't have much competition.

- **Tell the agent you want them to let it, too.** This is one to use with a good agent, especially if you're buying in an area you don't know well that's far away. If they know they'll get the lettings business, they're incentivised to find you a deal and ensure it's one that would rent easily.
- **Give feedback.** If you're not going to offer, tell them why: 'The second bedroom is too small to appeal to sharers', or 'It needs more work than I thought'. This gives them something to tell their client and is a potential hook for a lower offer.
- **Follow up deals.** Spied a good one that has already gone under offer? Nearly a fifth of sales fall through, so phone the agent every week until contracts are exchanged. If there is a hitch, you'll get their call. Failing that, you'll still stand out as a serious investor.

Buying agents

BFF or not, an estate agent works for the seller – not for you. You can, however, hire a buying agent to find a property for you and negotiate hard on your behalf, potentially saving you thousands of pounds. They will have clout with estate agents who know that they bring serious buyers, so can get you to the front of the queue. They can also source off-market deals and – this is probably their biggest advantage, especially when you're buying in an area you don't know – they'll know immediately what is a great deal and what isn't.

However, all this comes at a price. Most buying agents won't help you with purchases of under £500,000, and their fees are 1%–3% of the property's price. They usually charge an upfront deposit for a fixed search period of three to six months, with the rest of the fee due on completion of the sale. Vet buying agents carefully. A personal referral is best, as always, or look at industry awards and testimonials from previous clients.

How to choose a buying agent

Do:

- Ensure they have local knowledge
- Find an agent with whom you have rapport
- Ask to speak to other satisfied clients.

Don't:

- Be impressed by smart offices – you're paying for those
- Dawdle (the service stops after three to six months)
- Forget you have to pay their fees upon completion.

Sourcing companies

The poor(er) man's buying agent, sourcing companies find deals – often through negotiating bulk discounts with developers – and pass them on to their database of subscribers. There are no upfront fees; you only pay on completion, typically a flat fee of around £4,000.

If you're short on time, this could be a great option. However, it's not uncommon for multiple sourcers to peddle the same over-priced properties. So do your homework on the sourcing company itself. Armed with the methods we explain in this book, check that the price is really below market value and that the rental income would be as high as sourcers say. If the figures stack up and the sum of their fee plus the property's purchase price is still BMV, you're on to a good deal.

Auctions

Here's a trade secret for you: the top buying agents almost never buy at auction. Doing proper due diligence on all the lots you're interested in would cost a small fortune, only to lose out to a frenzy that pushes the price above market value on the day. The pros get better results through old-fashioned negotiation.

Nevertheless, the biggest plus of auctions is certainty – the deal is done when the hammer falls. You have to pay 10% on the day, and the rest within 28 days. If you take this route, here's the golden rule: *a property is sold at auction almost always because there is something wrong with it.* Find out what that is and how much it would cost to fix, then deduct that from the property's market value and bid no more.

There is one way to get that certainty without the heat of the moment: buy after the auction. The odd lot always goes unsold, probably because the undisclosed reserve price was not met. (That's not to be confused with the published guide price, which means zilch – it's often set unrealistically low to lure bids.) The owners may be open to offers afterwards, and if they accept yours, it's binding straight away as if you'd bought it under the gavel.

Our hearts said yes but the survey said no

We lost our hearts to an auction property once. It was a Victorian townhouse overlooking English Heritage's Marble Hill Park, in southwest London. Empty for perhaps a decade, this gem with its grand spaces and tall sash windows could become our forever home – or so we thought until 60 others with the same crush turned up at the first open viewing.

Nonetheless we paid for a £1,080 survey, which found the house had no foundations to speak of. Our builder put a renovation at £560,000. Worse, though, was the clawback clause buried in the legal documents: the buyer would have to pay the council, which originally owned the house, half of any profit when they sold the house on. Our romance was fading fast.

On the day of the auction, it sold to a banker and his interior designer wife for £952,000 – more than 50% above the guide price and well beyond the £830,000 we calculated as our maximum price. Almost five years on, the renovation is still not finished.

There are exceptions, though. At that same auction, a bog-standard Victorian terrace nearby – full of swirly carpets and flock wallpaper after its elderly owner had passed away – had almost no interest and sold on the day for £400,000. The buyer did absolutely nothing to the property and simply listed it with an estate agent, who sold the house within a week for £550,000. We're still kicking ourselves about that one.

What to look out for

Your buying checklist

The area:

- In an area that fits your tenant profile. Linger in your car and watch who comes and goes; peek into the surrounding front gardens. If you're targeting professionals, you want to see suits, shutters and skips
- Within 10 minutes from transport and shops (but not above a chippie or with the 7.45 from Slough rattling past at the bottom of the garden)
- Not on a busy road or with ugly views.

The property:

- The amount of bedrooms, bathrooms and outside space must suit your target tenant (see the tenant type table in Chapter 1 'How to avoid the No1 landlord mistake')
- First floor or secure ground floor, if it's a flat. Don't touch a basement or anything above the second floor without a lift

- Parking is a must for professionals outside London
- Tired condition but good layout, or the potential to create it. Could you just repaint and spruce up the kitchen with new cupboard doors?
- Double-glazing, a decent boiler and central heating will save you having to fit these yourself
- Damp smells and flaking paint, obvious slope or cracks (check if the upper floor's lintels are straight) and missing roof tiles spell trouble
- Well-kept common parts. Avoid a poorly run building
- Check that any extension had consent. If the neighbours have extended, there's a good chance you could, too
- Is there noise from upstairs neighbours? Visit at different times to check.

The circumstances:

- Check the lease length, service charges and ground rent (more on this below)
- Who lives there? If it's a tenant, will it be vacant? If it's the owner, have they found a new home? If it's empty, why – has it been done up, did the owner die or have they just moved out to sell?
- Why are they selling? 'Do not use' tape over the basin and loo signals repossession
- How long has it been on the market? Piles of post and knee-high grass mean a long time
- Have there been any offers? In estate agent speak, 'lots of interest' means no formal bids.

The last three questions are the most important – and you're more likely to find answers from the agent if you view in person.

To negotiate the best deal, *start by making an offer that you know will get rejected*. Yes, really. This should be lower than your maximum offer, but will help you gauge the seller's minimum. Sell your offer to them: speed and certainty count. If you're bidding against other buyers, raise your offer substantially – say, by £10,000 – to seal the deal. If your bid is rejected, leave it on the table and follow up weekly until contracts are exchanged.

Which survey should you use? A HomeBuyer report (£300–£500) is enough for most purchases; do a full Building Survey only if you're buying a building that's listed, old or of non-standard construction such as concrete. Surveyors tend to cover their backsides in their written reports, pointing out even the smallest risks. It helps to get chummy and ask them over the phone what is really worth worrying about.

Don't skimp on a solicitor – a bad one could cost you the deal – and gently chase them along. As in life, the squeaky wheel gets the grease. Solicitors are busy and can take weeks to notice that the answer to one specific query is still not in, unless you prod.

Buying a leasehold flat

As if buying property was not complex enough, buying a leasehold flat adds a whole new layer of complication. We could write a book about lease pitfalls, but here are 10 of the most common issues to look out for:

1. **How long is the lease?** It's expensive to renew if it's below 80 years, and impossible to get a mortgage if the lease is under 60ish years. (See the previous chapter for how to renew it.)
2. **What are the service charges?** This annual fee, which covers the buildings insurance and maintenance costs for the structure and common parts, can vary hugely. For a one-bedroom flat in a small, well-run block, £1,000 is reasonable.
3. **Beware the trimmings...**Lifts, underground parking, a concierge or ornate period exteriors will push up service charges to as much as £5,000 a year for a one-bedder.
4. **...and beware the too trim.** No service charge, or a very low one, suggests the building is badly run. Expect a whopper of a bill down the line.

5. **Are payments up to date?** If the seller owes any service charges, you'll be liable for that debt.
6. **How much is the ground rent?** Watch out for 'staircased' ground rent that rises every few years, payable to the freeholder.
7. **Check the lease terms.** Are there any nasty restrictions on, for example, letting out your flat?
8. **Is there a sinking fund?** Larger blocks should have a savings reserve built up from part of the service charge to pay for large maintenance projects.
9. **Are major works planned?** If so, and in the absence of a sinking fund, there's a big collection round the corner.
10. **Has there been past subsidence?** Shifting foundations would mean high buildings insurance premiums and therefore high service charges.

Buying off-plan

New build flats in London rent for 40% more than older equivalents in the same area, reports CBRE property group. Tenants like the energy efficiency and low maintenance. There's also no chain when you buy off-plan, and you usually get a 10-year guarantee should any defects arise because the builder didn't comply with industry standards. Plus, it may make financial sense: you usually put down a 10% deposit on exchange of contract, with the rest due at completion. That means you buy at today's price, but you have time until tomorrow to raise the finance. However, if values fall before the property is built, you could have a black hole on your balance sheet (see anecdote).

Avoid buying in huge new build developments where an oversupply of similar properties hits the market all at once. You may struggle to let or sell and could be forced to cut your price after paying a premium for all that shininess. Only buy off-plan in low-volume boutique developments and study plans carefully to avoid, for example, being overshadowed by a large building. Secure a property in the first batch of sales. The best ones sell first and will achieve the highest future resale prices. Beware, too, of discounts or offers by developers to pay your stamp duty – that usually means the purchase price is just slightly less inflated.

£14,000 off-plan loss turns out to be great escape

Daniel once burnt his fingers on an off-plan purchase. It was a two-bedroom flat in a converted silk mill in the sleepy West Yorkshire town of Elland, near Leeds, advertised as a 'below market value' deal for £149,000 in 2007. Daniel, still without his sceptical journalist wife, exchanged contracts. A year later, the global financial crisis took hold. Having still not completed, Daniel feared he wouldn't get a mortgage and pulled out of the purchase – losing £14,000. Had the sale gone through, his loss would have been far greater: eight years after the crash, those flats still sell for no more than about £110,000. The mortgage payments would have been £660 a month, while the flats now rent for about £450 due to an oversupply – despite the exposed brickwork and country views that tempted him to buy in the first place. That would have forced him to fork out £210 a month while being in negative equity. Phew, that was a close call.

Buying a property that is already let

Tenants in situ mean you're buying income from day one and you won't have costs to fill the place yourself. However, they bring uncertainty: are you taking on good tenants? Are there any disputes that you don't know of? That's why many landlords like to start with a clean slate. Also, some lenders won't offer you a buy-to-let mortgage when tenants are already living in the property, so ask your broker about this upfront.

If you do plan to buy with tenants in situ, it's worth asking these 10 questions:

1. What type of tenancy agreement is in place? Steer clear of anything that is not an assured shorthold tenancy

2. How long is left on the contract, and are you happy with all the terms?
3. Are there any rent arrears?
4. Is the deposit protected and was the prescribed information issued?
5. How long have the tenants been at the property?
6. Is it possible to meet the tenants? Gut feeling is a good indicator.
7. What reference checks were taken for the tenants, and do they have guarantors?
8. Are there any disputes with neighbours over antisocial behaviour?
9. Has there ever been a pest infestation?
10. Are you liable for any fees payable to a letting agent for the current tenants?

Once you've bought the property, by law you must write to tell the tenants that you are their new landlord and supply an address in England or Wales where they can give notice. (It can be your lettings agent's address.) Ask them to change their standing order for rent to go to your account. You can offer them a new tenancy agreement but they don't have to accept.

There's a heck of a lot of detail here and, when buying, it's easy to get lost in that. But to buy successfully, focus on the big things: get your financing in place up front. Buy with selling in mind, even if that's decades down the line. And never lose sight of your goal – no matter how good a deal it is, if a property won't give you what you want, it's not the one for you.

CHAPTER 18

How to sell your rental property

In this chapter:

- **Should I sell with my tenant in situ? Plus other key questions before you sell**
- **Seven steps to achieve the highest possible sale price**
- **When to use an estate agent for your sale – and when to do it yourself.**

You may well have heard someone lament that they'd be a gazillionnaire by now if only they hadn't sold that flat in Hackney back in 1991. (That once-scruffy East End spot, by the way, has seen the fastest rising house prices in Britain over the past three decades.) And, fair enough, most investors will finance their next purchase by remortgaging to access equity – not by selling. But despite the 'hold forever' mantra, there could be good reasons to sell your rental property.

Why sell the goose that lays the golden eggs? Those eggs may not be quite as golden as you had hoped – or they were, but you think things are about to change if the area's prices are flat-lining, so you could do better elsewhere. Perhaps your goals have changed: you may have needed income so you could start a business but now you're after price growth to fund your retirement. Or you simply need the cash to buy a home of your own.

In this section we cover the key questions to ask before you start the sales process, how to get the highest possible price and whether or not you should use an agent.

Three key questions before you sell

Before you open Rightmove to see how much flats like yours sell for, start by answering three crucial questions:

1. **Is the timing right for capital gains tax?** Speak to an accountant or tax specialist to find out. A married couple who are joint owners could save more than £6,000 just by ensuring a sale goes through in the right tax year. Depending on your other tax liabilities, gifting your spouse a share of the property ahead of the sale could be a wise move (see Chapter 4 'Think ahead to save a fortune in tax').

2. **When can I give my tenants notice?** Check your tenancy agreement to see when the fixed term ends, as you cannot force your tenants to leave before then (see Chapter 12 'The nuts and bolts of ending a tenancy'). They may agree to leave early, but then again you may want to sell with them staying on. Speaking of which...

3. **Should I sell with my tenant in situ?** Talk to a few good local agents to find out whether you should sell with your tenant in situ. The answer depends on who would be your likely buyer. If your property would appeal mainly to investors – for example, if it's a studio flat – keeping a good tenant means they get income from day one. As a bonus, the rent will cover your mortgage ahead of the sale, and you won't have to pay council tax or higher insurance premiums while it's empty.

   In a family home, however, tenants in situ will deter the bulk of your market: people who buy to live there themselves. You won't be able to dress the house, and viewings can be a pain if the tenants give you a hard time.

You (or your lettings agent) could speak to your tenants: they may want to buy the house themselves. Even if they don't, you still need to get them on board for viewing access. They pay for their right to peace and quiet, and can make your sale all but impossible if they're not treated with respect.

Seven steps to sell for more

How do you achieve the highest possible selling price? Your ideal scenario is where two (or more) buyers enter into a bidding war. That won't happen with wily investors, but it could if owner-occupiers lose their hearts – and heads – to your home.

Here's how to make that happen:

1. **Have selling in mind from the start.** When you buy, ask yourself: 'Just because I like it, will someone else like it, too?' You may be willing to live in a dark basement flat on a busy road, but many other buyers won't. Ditto for ex-council flats or properties far from a station (or right next to one). Likewise, let the wants of your likely buyer guide to which spec you refurb your property. There's no point in putting in your dream spa bath if most of your market would prefer a walk-in shower.
2. **Take professional photos.** It never ceases to amaze us that people plough six figures into their biggest asset yet settle for a lazy agent's blurry smartphone shots to market it to the world. Paying £100 for a photographer to make it look its best will let your property stand out by a mile online.
3. **Stage your property.** There's a reason why developers do show homes: they create a vision of living there. One investor we know does up and tastefully decorates period flats – selling with every hand-printed linen cushion in place for as much as £20,000 more than she'd get without the trimmings. You can rent or buy a complete furniture pack from home staging companies, or use one of their designers to style what you have.

   At the very least, follow the same tips as for preparing your property to let (see Chapter 6 'Prep and promote your property') and add a few aspirational touches – be it bottles of artisan olive oil and balsamic in the kitchen, or a bistro set outside so buyers can picture themselves having brunch on your sunny terrace.

4. **Price just below the going rate.** To value your property, use the same process that we explain under 'How to assess market value' in the previous chapter. Once you know the going rate, price your property about £5,000 lower. Beautifully staged and professionally photographed, at that price it will get feet through the door and, with a bit of luck, spark a bidding war.

   Beware of agents who overvalue your sale price just to get the business. If you overprice, this is what usually happens: your property will sit on the market for a while, with little or no interest. Buyers will start thinking there's something wrong with it. Your agent will tell you to knock down the price – and you'll have to drop it quite a bit, not just £5,000. In the end, you may well sell for less than you'd have got if you'd priced it right from the start. As one estate agent friend likes to say: 'Like hot cakes, hot property goes cold when on the market for too long.'

5. **Don't give away too much.** Don't tell your agent why you're selling, or they will almost certainly let it slip to the buyer. To them, it's a bit of juicy gossip that will bag them their commission; to you it's thousands of lost pounds. If the buyer asks about your reasons, be vague ('it seems like the right time') – it's not on the list of questions you are obliged to answer.

6. **Listen to feedback.** Are buyers saying, 'The house is too small'? It means they can get a bigger place for the same money – so drop your price. If they comment that 'it looks a bit tired', it's time to clean the carpets, repaint the scuffs and replace those dated kitchen door handles. A test viewing with your tidiest friend could highlight anything off-putting.

7. **Chase the deal through.** Once the offer has been agreed, keep chasing the agent and solicitors: the transaction is not binding until contracts are exchanged. Almost one in five transactions in England (about 200,000) fall through each year, costing consumers £270 million annually, government figures show.

   Besides ensuring that the deal goes through, staying on top of things will speed it up – saving you thousands in holding costs. For the same reason, have all your paperwork on guarantees, insurance and building control ready to hand over as soon as the buyer's solicitor asks for it.

It may be worth accepting a cash buyer or someone who is not in a chain, even if their offer is slightly lower, as that will make the transaction much likelier to go through.

Do you need an agent?

As with letting your property, the new generation of online agents lets you advertise your house on the big portals from as little as £500 – saving you tens of thousands of pounds in commission. This is a good option if the market is buoyant and you have good comparables to help you value your property – and, crucially, demonstrate to a buyer that your price is realistic. You won't, however, have access to an agent's database of registered buyers. If it takes longer to sell, your holding costs may wipe out the saving on fees.

Importantly, if you sell your property yourself, you need to keep nudging the solicitors along. Without an agent to harass them, your transaction will quietly slip to the bottom of their pile while you still have to pay the mortgage on your empty property.

How we saved £10,000 by selling our flat ourselves

When the time came to sell our Wimbledon ex-council flat, the estate agent from whom Daniel had bought it quoted 1.75% in commission to flog it again. However, the neighbour, whom Daniel knew well, had just sold their almost identical three-bedroom flat for £390,000 after receiving several offers. The market was busy, so we decided to sell via an online agent for a fixed fee of £600.

While our tenants were still in situ, we asked for their permission to take professional marketing photos – for which we styled the flat using cushions and bed linen from our main home. The very first couple who viewed made an offer and, based on the neighbour's sale, we persuaded them to raise their price to the same level. Selling it ourselves had saved us about £7,000 in commission fees.

However, we did lose out on at least a month's rent because of delays in what should have been a straightforward chain-free sale. Had we used a better solicitor – not an online conveyancing service – and questioned more when the buyers said their financing was 'sorted' (which should mean they have a mortgage offer in principle, not just that they've called a broker), we'd have been £1,000 or so better off. Don't scrimp on solicitors and chase every few days to make sure the sale goes through.

If you do decide to use a traditional estate agent, appoint only one – it appears desperate and confusing to buyers if the same property is on with too many agents. The typical commission for a sole agent is 2%, compared to 3.5% for multiple or two joint sole agents. To get the best out of an agent, appoint them for the minimum term – usually four weeks – and incentivise them with a bonus if they sell for above a certain price.

A third option is to sell via auction (2.5% plus £300–£1,500 for your catalogue advert). This is quick and easy: the sale becomes binding as soon as the hammer falls, and all the money is in your pocket after 28 days. Once the preserve of investors in white vans, auction parking lots are now filled with the crossover hatchbacks of families weaned on a decade of *Homes Under The Hammer.* Auctions work particularly well for quirky properties like canal-side cottages.

Whichever route you choose to sell through, one truth applies: between you and your buyer, whoever looks more desperate will lose out. Get your price right, don't reveal your reasons for selling and make it easy for a buyer to get smitten with your house – then the winner will be you.

Now, here's your big challenge

You are already one of a select few. Less than 5% of adults in Britain own a rental property – and you can count yourself among them. But if you get strategic with your property, you'll be truly exceptional.

Like you (and like us), more than half of that 5% used to live in their property, or they inherited it, according to a representative buy-to-let survey by Opinion Matters. In other words, they started out as accidental landlords. Yet one in two remain accidental landlords in the sense that they have no written business plan, the same survey shows.

You may have started this book as an accidental landlord, but we've done everything we can to ensure you don't have to stay one. We've shown you the importance of putting the big things in place first: the goal you want to reach, the plan to get you there, and the means for it in the form of the right financing. We've taken you step by step through the five Ps of the lettings process, so you'll be prepared for anything – and have peace of mind that you've done all you should. And we've given you a vision beyond this property, to use it as a first step towards a portfolio that can fund the life you want.

The key to making a success of letting out your home – whatever that success looks like to you – is to move from accidental to deliberate. Do you want to build a portfolio? Then you need to choose your next property deliberately so you can tap into its value to finance another. Would you rather pocket a lump sum? That may take a deliberate refurb aimed at a target buyer. Or do you simply want the rent every month and your home back in good shape? Even that means being deliberate in how you prepare your property, choose tenants and manage the let.

Most importantly, an ethical landlord is a deliberate one. We give our tenants shelter – a basic human need – and we do this in a market where many of them are priced out of owning their home. Our decisions can have a profound impact on families who, say, can't afford the higher rent and then have to uproot their children from school. Beyond our legal duty to provide a safe home, we also have a duty to deliberate on how we affect our tenants' lives.

In this book we've given you the tools to do all this. So here's your challenge: be one of the deliberate few. Act on what you've learnt to make the most of your property. It's not easy – that's why we've filled 18 chapters on it – but it's entirely doable and it brings great rewards, financial and otherwise.

Get the free extras

We've put together some practical tools in digital form, so you can amend, email and print them as needed.

It's all completely free, with no strings attached. To access the following, all you need to do is register with your email address (and we promise we won't spam you – we hate that as much as most people do):

- **Your all-in-one checklist:** an electronic version of our full list of everything you need to do when you start letting out your home, as given at the beginning of this book. Let the box-ticking commence!
- **House guide:** a manual for your tenants on how to use your home. It covers emergencies, maintenance problems and everything you expect them to do – which will spare you costly repair bills and silly call-outs on Christmas Eve.
- **Tenant check-out list.** Around six weeks before your tenants move out, email them this detailed list of how they should leave the property to avoid deductions. This will save you no end of deposit wrangles, so you can part on good terms.

For instant free access, sign up at **accidentallandlord.info/extras**.

Glossary

Accidental landlord: an owner who lets out their home without having bought it as a rental investment. Some do so after a change in job, partner or country; others inherit a property, or struggle to sell so temporarily let instead.

Applicant: someone seeking to rent a property. Once the tenancy starts, they become a tenant.

Assured shorthold tenancy (AST): the most common form of tenancy, which gives you an automatic right to take your property back at the end of the fixed term stated in the contract.

Betterment: if your tenant breaks your old Ikea sofa with their best Tom Cruise impression, you can't deduct the price of a sleek new corner unit from their deposit. You can't end up better off than you would have been if fair wear and tear applied.

Below market value (BMV): usually not the deals advertised as 'BMV opportunities', but below market value sales do exist – prices of identical properties can differ because of circumstances such as useless marketing or a bidding war. Your job is to assess the true market value: is the owner desperate, or is there a hidden flaw?

Break clause: a negotiable clause in your contract that allows you or your tenant to end the tenancy before the fixed term is up.

Buy-to-let mortgage: a property loan based mainly on the rental income, not your personal earnings. You need a deposit of at least 25% and the rent must cover 125%-145% of the mortgage payments, though rules may tighten up.

Build-to-rent: developments built to rent out to private tenants. Aimed at lifestyle renters, they tend to be swish – think rooftop bars and pet grooming stations – and are professionally let and managed by companies. Now still a small part of the private rental sector, these will be your competition in years to come.

Capital gains tax: the tax on the gain when you sell or transfer a property that has risen in value. Accidental landlords get quite a few tax breaks – see Chapter 4 'Think ahead to save a fortune in tax'.

Check-in: on move-in day, you – or your inventory clerk – meet your tenant at the property to hand over keys, sign the inventory and do a quick tour, pointing out the mains switches.

Check-out: at the end of the tenancy, the tenant can simply leave all keys inside the property and close the door. You, or an independent clerk, take final meter readings and compare the contents and condition of the property to the check-in inventory. This can happen with or without the tenants present.

Client money protection: the law will soon require agents to keep tenants' and landlords' money in an account separate from that of their firm. If this is not in place and the agency goes bust, their creditors can take your money.

Consent to let: if you have a residential mortgage but want to rent out your property temporarily, you must ask your lender's consent. Not doing so is mortgage fraud and could cause them to call in the loan. Yes, that does happen.

Council tax: the tenant pays council tax to the local authority during the tenancy; you pay it when the property is empty.

Deposit: not a free bonus to fund a Caribbean cruise, sorry. The deposit money belongs to the tenant, but you, or your agent, hold it as security against property damage (excluding fair wear and tear) and unpaid rent. By law you must protect the deposit in a government-backed scheme.

DSS: the Department of Social Security of old, which used to run welfare payments. Often used in lettings adverts, 'DSS' really means tenants on housing benefit.

Electrical installation report: it's good practice for an electrician to check the main wiring every five years. This will likely become law from 2017 and is already a requirement for any property let to three or more sharers.

Energy performance certificate (EPC): rates how draughty or cosy your home is so tenants can see upfront if heating bills are likely to be high. By law, you need an EPC to market your property for rent or sale. You must wave it about throughout the lettings process (see Chapter 7 'Tick the legal boxes') and give your tenant a copy before they move in, otherwise you lose your automatic right to get your property back.

Equity: the amount you'd get back if you sold your home and repaid the mortgage. It includes your deposit, capital you've repaid and any gains in price.

Freehold: if you own the freehold, you own the building and the land it stands on outright with no time limit.

Gas safety certificate: so your tenants won't be blown to smithereens, an engineer on the Gas Safe register must test the gas supply and all gas appliances in your rented property before the start of the first let and then once a year. You also have to give your tenants a copy of the certificate. Forget this and you could face heavy fines.

Guarantor: someone who guarantees that they will pay the rent and fulfil any other duties listed in the contract if the tenant defaults. Insist on a working homeowner (or two) as guarantor.

House in multiple occupation (HMO): where three or more people who don't form a single household share a kitchen or bathroom, for example a group of friends sharing a house, a student house, or a house let by room. Rules vary depending on the area – see Chapter 7 'Tick the legal boxes'.

HMRC: the taxman – full name Her Majesty's Revenue & Customs.

Inventory: a detailed written record with photos of the contents and condition of the property. Get an independent clerk to compile it, otherwise you won't have much of a case in any deposit dispute.

Jointly and severally liable: if there is more than one tenant, each person is 'jointly and severally liable' for the full rent. That means if one leaves or stops paying, the others still have to pay the full amount (not just their portion) for the rest of the term. That's quite a commitment for sharers.

Landlord licensing: one in ten councils in England and the whole of Wales and Scotland have brought in selective licensing for landlords. That means you have to pay around £500 per property for a five-year licence that requires you to do the stuff you're probably doing anyway: contracts, references and safety checks (most of which are already legislated). We'll resist the strong temptation to swear at this point; read our full rant in Chapter 7 'Tick the legal boxes'.

Leasehold: you 'rent' the property (usually a flat) and its land for a very long period stated in the lease – often 125 years, but sometimes as long as 999 years. When the lease expires you have to hand the keys to the building's owner, called the freeholder.

Legionella: the bacterium found in standing water that can cause Legionnaires' Disease – a potentially fatal form of pneumonia. You must assess the risk of Legionella breeding in your property's water system.

Leverage: how borrowing, also called gearing, catapults your property returns (or losses, watch out) from ordinary to phenomenal. As the word suggests, it acts like a lever: if you apply a small force (your deposit) to a lever (your mortgage), it amplifies the effect (your return).

Loan-to-value (LTV): shown as a percentage, this is the amount you borrow (the loan) as a proportion of the property's value. If you put down a 15% deposit, the loan-to-value will be 85%.

Non-resident landlord tax: if you live abroad, your agent or tenant has a legal obligation to deduct tax from rent before they pay it into your account. To avoid errors, apply for an HMRC approved number – then the full rent can be paid to you, allowing you to make the most of expenses and allowances.

Notice period: how long in advance the landlord or tenant has to warn the other party that they are ending the tenancy.

PAT test: you don't have to do portable appliance testing (PAT) on the kettle or toaster, but you must ensure they are safe to use and at least have the CE safety mark. To cover yourself, it's best not to supply small appliances.

Period property: usually refers to Victorian, Georgian or Edwardian architecture – generally anything built more than a century ago.

Periodic tenancy: a statutory periodic tenancy is one that rolls on month by month or week by week, depending on how you've charged rent so far. You don't have to re-sign the initial contract but all its terms still apply, except that you or your tenant can now give notice any time.

Possession: taking back your property. You can only do this through a set legal process, not by calling your beefy brother-in-law to change the locks.

Prescribed information: paperwork that explains how the deposit is protected. You must give this to your tenant within 30 days of receiving the money, or face a fine and lose your right to take your house back at the end of the fixed term. Confusingly, 'prescribed information' can also refer to the government's 'How To Rent' leaflet, which you must give to your tenant before they move in.

Renewal: when the tenancy's initial fixed term ends, you can renew the contract for a further fixed term – in other words, start over and sign the paperwork again. This is the best time to negotiate a rent rise.

Rent-a-room Scheme: if you let out a furnished room in your home to a lodger – or even a whole floor (but not a separate flat or the entire place) – you can earn up to £7,500 a year tax free by opting into HMRC's Rent-a-room Scheme.

Return on investment (ROI): a formula that shows how hard your money is working. Divide your net annual rental income by the total cash you've invested in the property, then turn the answer into a percentage.

Right to Rent: you must check that tenants have the right to live and work in Britain before letting a property to them – or face a penalty of up to £3,000 per adult illegal immigrant living there, even if they are not named in the lease. You can thank the European migrant crisis for that one.

Section 8: one of two kinds of notices you can serve to warn your tenant that you are ending the tenancy. It says that your tenant has committed a serious breach and you want them out, but this requires you to pick one or more reasons (or 'grounds for possession', such as rent arrears) from a pre-written list. You must be able to prove the breach in court. Don't issue this lightly, if at all.

Section 21: the second – and far easier – type of notice you can serve to tell your tenant you are ending the tenancy. It's a way of saying that the tenant hasn't done anything wrong, but you want your house back anyway (which you have an automatic right to). You can use this route only at the end of the fixed term stated in your contract, or thereafter if the tenancy has rolled on. You must have followed the law precisely throughout the tenancy.

Service charges: an annual fee you pay to the freeholder of almost any flat. It covers the buildings insurance and maintenance costs for the structure and common parts. Before you buy, check what this is so you're not clobbered.

Sinking fund: nothing to do with sinking, it's a savings reserve built up from part of the service charge to pay for large maintenance projects.

Subsidence: everything to do with sinking. Shifting foundations caused by underground water, tree roots or structural defects.

Surrender: white flag optional. This is when your tenant gives up the property before the end of the fixed term and you accept their surrender.

Tenancy agreement: a contract between landlord and tenant setting out the rent, fixed term (if any) and legal conditions.

Void: avoid at all costs, with the exception of a bad tenant. It's an empty period when you get no rent but still have to pay the mortgage.

Yield: a very rough way to measure income success. Divide the annual rent by the price you paid for the property, then turn the answer into a percentage. When someone says 'yield', they normally mean gross yield before expenses are deducted, so take their claims with a shovel of salt. Net yield, on the other hand, takes costs into account.

Index

A

B

C

D

E

F

G

H

I

J

K

L

M

N

O

P

Acknowledgements

Daniel would like to acknowledge Swift's clients and all the accidental landlords he has worked with over the years. It is only through them that he has the experience – and the arsenal of anecdotes – to write *The Accidental Landlord*.

Martina would like to thank Helen Davies, *Home* editor of *The Sunday Times*, and her newspaper colleagues at Britain's best-selling property section for their generous support as she crafted her first book and, in the years before, a career as a property journalist.

Thank you to Sandi Durnford-Slater, Jonathan Moss, Susan Peacock and Jens Wittrowski for their invaluable feedback on our first draft. Jon Cooper, director of CooperFaure accountants, made sure we got our tax facts straight , while Robert Shaw, our trusted adviser from R W Mortgage Solutions, did likewise on mortgages. Lucy McCarraher, Joe Gregory and the team at Rethink Press have been outstanding as they polished and published our words.

And lastly, but most importantly, thank you to our two Leeslets aged under three – the youngest born half way through writing this book – who patiently put up with many hours of watching Mamma and Pappa type.

The authors

Daniel Lees and **Martina Lees** became accidental landlords when they got married and decided to let out Daniel's former bachelor pad in Southfields, southwest London. Eight years on – having travelled the world, bought a family home and grown a small buy-to-let portfolio funded in part by that bachelor flat – they still haven't stopped talking about property.

After friends who were moving abroad asked **Daniel** to rent out their Southfields flat, he founded Swift Property (swift.property) as a specialist, independent lettings agency in 2010. Clients in thirteen countries across five continents have since trusted Swift to let and manage their properties in southwest London. Almost all of them are accidental landlords who used to live in – and still love – these homes, and 95% chose Swift based on word-of-mouth recommendations. Along the way, Swift has resolved hundreds of callouts, once even needing to rescue a pet python from a leak.

Martina is a property journalist and columnist at the Home section of *The Sunday Times*, the best-selling property newspaper section in Britain. She has won LSL Property Press awards for her coverage, including a 12-page guide on buy-to-let and an interview with Eric Clapton on the rock star's £2.6 million villa in Provence. Ahead of the 2015 election, Martina's three-month investigation showed how Britain's housing crisis affects us all. Lord Richard Best, the veteran housing campaigner, said Martina 'may have helped change events post-election'.

Download your free extras to this book, including a tenant house guide and an all-in-one checklist, at accidentallandlord.info/extras. Follow us on Twitter at @AccLandlord and @SwiftLettings.